# WHEN LIFE HANDS YOU CACTUSES, MAKE MARGARITAS

## BY ADIBA BARNEY

*Published and distributed in the United States by Life Lessons Publishing*

**Author** Adiba Barney

**Interior Design** Grade Design and Adeline Media, London

**Cover Design** Heather Schellhase Strianese, Leveret Paperie

**Cover Photography** Angie Lamia Jacoby, Jacoby Rose Photography

**Content Creation Services** StoryTerrace

**Copyright** © Adiba Barney

**All rights reserved.**

First print October 2020

**Paperback ISBN** 978-1-7349290-2-7

**E-Book ISBN** 978-1-7349290-3-4

# DEDICATION

Living with a deadly disease like metastatic breast cancer can be a very lonely existence. However, since I'm surrounded by so many incredible people who love and support me no matter what, I never get to be alone in this… even if I wanted to.

That's why I want to dedicate this book to so many.

To the light of my life, my precious son Alex.
To the love of my life, my hero husband Kris.

To my cheerleaders and helping hands and hearts: my mom and dad, my sisters and their husbands, my brother, my mother and father in-law, and my brothers and sisters-in-law. To my girl tribes, my besties in Sweden, and in the U.S.

You hold me up high when I feel the lowest. You make me laugh with joy, and you cry with me when I'm sad. You give me space to vent when I need it and a hand that both holds and helps. You go on crazy fun trips and adventures with me, and you let me be who I am.

I love you, and I'm forever grateful to you.
Adiba

# TABLE OF CONTENTS

# FOREWORD

I still vividly remember the first time my wife and I met, now more than nine years ago. Life since then has been full of more curveballs and challenges than I ever imagined, but we've persevered, in large part due to Adiba's continual optimism and tenacity (she definitely hasn't lost an ounce of either since we met!).

Cancer is a force of perpetual destruction, and it takes the resolve of someone truly amazing to battle it each and every day. I'm certainly biased, but I can't think of a person I admire more than my wife. She approaches every roadblock life throws at her with strength and positivity, no matter how challenging or difficult it may be. And she does this on top of being an amazing mother to our son Alex (whom we treasure, but at two years old, can definitely be a handful at times!).

The three of us will keep fighting to continue "writing the story of her life" for decades to come (nothing would make us happier than needing to update this book a decade from now!). I couldn't be happier to help her share her story with the world. After reading this book, I'm sure you will agree that my wife's story, thus far, is nothing short of inspiring!

As always, your support, thoughts, and prayers are much appreciated!

Kris Barney

October 2020

# PREFACE

Where should I start? Well, writing this book is both a pain and a liberation. Why? Because as I look back over my life, I see many years of struggle as well as many years filled with joy and pride.

Pride in what I've been able to accomplish through all the tough years, and true joy for life I've felt, but also pain for time lost to numerous struggles and sorrows.

I've always been a strong soul, I think, starting from the time I was born. Surely the years filled with challenges have helped me find a way to not let them get to me, to not be worn down by them, and not allow me to fall into any dark holes.

The fact is, despite my challenges, I've also had a very fun, successful and inspiring career, three great love stories, and amazing and caring family and friends who have helped me throughout my journey.

So, why am I writing a book about my life? This book is for me, my son, and it's for you.

Me, because I need to cherish and celebrate the life I have had and still have before it is taken from me. My son, because he will most likely lose me way too soon. I believe hearing my story in my words will help him face and manage his grief. And you, because maybe, just maybe, you will find inspiration from my journey and ways to handle your own challenges in life.

Adiba Barney
October 2020

# PROLOGUE

The sirens went off — *Hurry!* Hide! My mom, super preggo with me and almost ready to burst, held my father's hand as he held my brother in his arms. Together, they ran for shelter as the bombs steadily rained down. The shelter was across the street and two floors underground from the house we had called home. We lived underground for weeks, sometimes months at a time, when the bombing was constant. During those times, living underground was the only way we could survive.

It was 1977 in Beirut, Lebanon and the civil war had already been going on there for two years. The war lasted from 1975 until 1990 and ended with an estimated 120,000 fatalities, or 7% of the population. Almost one million people emigrated from Lebanon as a result of the war.

*Holy shit!* My mother's water breaks, spilling onto the floor where my mom, dad and brother were hiding. They were trembling with fear, waiting for this one to pass (the bomb raid, that is, not me). It's dark. The screams and cries, along with the bombs hitting their targets, drowned out my mom's screams from each contraction's shooting pain – she's coming!!!

The pain was too much for my mom to bear. My dad had a look of fear in his eyes, not from the bombs falling outside, but because it was difficult for him to see his beloved wife in such agony. "Please, is there anyone who knows how to deliver a baby?" he shouted. A woman, who normally worked as a doula in the neighborhood, appeared, "I can help." After hours of trying, it turned out that I didn't want to come out into that horrific world. The umbilical cord had wrapped itself around my neck. My mom needed to get to a hospital immediately or else she would lose me and herself in the process.

A friendly neighbor and his family lived close by. Dad knew that their car was still functional, hidden behind a concrete wall in their building's garage – but how would he get to it? My dad ran, carrying my mom as my brother held on tight to his back, until they finally reached the neighbor's shelter. The neighbor showed kindness and offered to give them a ride to the nearest hospital. They traveled through the city as the bombs were coming down, somehow managing to avoid them. Luckily, my mom was in too much pain to even notice.

# OCTOBER 23, 1977

I was born that day by emergency C-section, amazingly, with the whole family alive and well. As they looked at me, the tiny monkey who had come out, they saw that I was covered in body hair called Lanugo, a soft, fine hair that sometimes covers a baby and acts as a protectant in the womb. Man, I must have known that I needed protection.

That is, my dear friends, how I came into this world. Little did I know that the very moment of my birth would pave the way for a strength and resilience that would prove crucial for what was to come.

Welcome to the story of my life…

# WHY CACTUSES AND MARGARITAS?

The word "cactus" derives from the Latin, kaktos, meaning spiny plant whose identity is not certain.

I feel connected to the cactus due to its endurance and ability to thrive in challenging environments. A cactus is adaptable and strong, just like me. Its resilient capabilities are its real beauty. The beauty that originates from the inside.

The margarita represents another side of who I am. It represents my immense love and passion for living life. A life filled with fun, adventures, and love despite the hardship.

With the title of this book, I wanted to marry the two: cactuses and margaritas.

I live my life like there is no tomorrow and like I'm gonna live forever.

# RESILIENCE IS THE KEY

My whole life experience can be summarized with one word: resilience. I've had to be resilient and strong many times throughout my life, as you will read about in this book. After each time, I gained more self-knowledge, new tools, and ways of handling the stress, pain, and grief that comes with each challenge and tragedy.

I am resilient, but that doesn't mean I don't break down sometimes. I'm only human after all, even though I wish I was superhuman. I always allowed myself to feel all the numerous emotions that came with each breakdown. By being resilient over and over again, I've learned how to work through those emotions and not let them bring me down into a dark and sad place. Most importantly, if I ever ventured into that dark place, I never stayed. I have always gotten out of it and lived my life.

I personally believe that anyone can be resilient and strong. It is not something that you're either born with or not. Resilience develops along the journey of life. It develops when you know more about yourself and truly respect, love, and believe in yourself. Having a positive view of yourself and confidence in your abilities and strength is key.

Another really important part of my journey, and how I am able to follow my own margarita recipe, is that I don't really give a shit about the little things. Things, happenings in life that normally take up too much space in people's minds and hearts, just don't bother me. I won't let them. After all, if it's not a death or life situation, it is always fixable and not the whole world, you know?

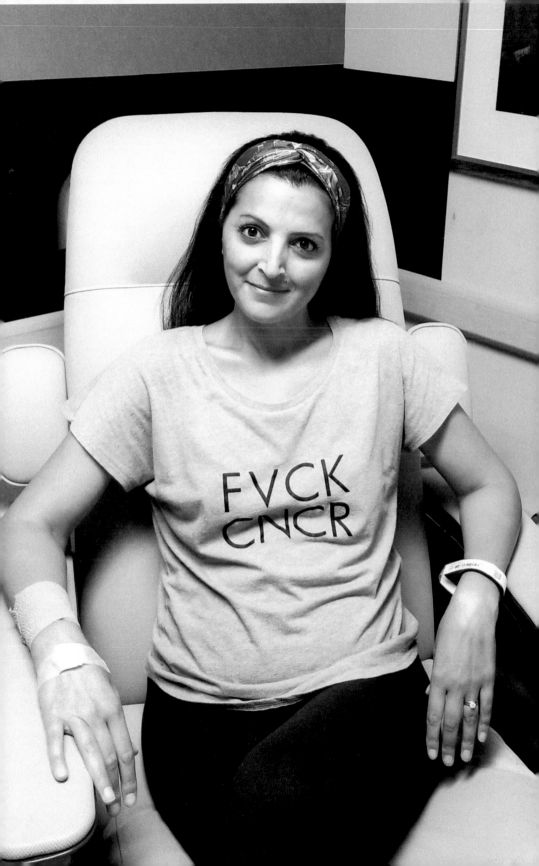

# 1

## CHILD OF WAR:
### WHERE DID MY CHILDHOOD GO?

I was born into a terrifying world where bombs constantly rained down all around. For the first seven years of my life, this was the only existence I knew. These years were far from what most people would ever experience during a typical childhood. I was surrounded by so much tragedy during this time. Many of my parents' friends died. Entire families were killed. I experienced unspeakable terror and trauma at such an early age. Most of it I don't remember, even from the age when most children do start remembering. I can recall a few fragments here and there, but they feel more like dreams or nightmares really, and not actual events. My mom and dad have told me about our life during those years, the parts that I've suppressed deep in my brain somewhere — a place that I dared not open even when I returned to visit Beirut, Lebanon, for the first time in September 2016, after we fled in 1984.

The war had an unforgettable and lasting impact on the early years of my life. One of the most terrifying memories I have from the war is waking up abruptly, because the wall next to my bed was shaking hard from the bombs that were coming down. I remember my whole body trembling and feeling as if my heart was in my throat, terrified that they would hit our building next. Knowing we had mere moments before that could happen, we fled our home, taking only what we could hold in our arms, and ran across the street to the entrance of the underground shelter, hoping we would make it to safety in time.

Safety for us was a cramped, stuffy underground room where we lived for weeks, sometimes months, at a time. There were nonstop noises, inside and out. We ate whatever canned food we could come by, passing the days while the bombing continued outside our windowless space. It was even dangerous to venture out to get water from the well that was only 100 meters (328 feet) from the shelter. To get it meant that someone had to run to the well, retrieve the water, and get back while avoiding the bombs. My dad narrowly escaped being hit on several occasions while getting water for us. Our goal was to survive, and we did everything possible to make sure we did. We held tight to the hope that we would survive, somehow.

In the shelter, us kids had to learn how to creatively play in small spaces with whatever toy we had been able to bring with us. The adults also found ways to occupy their time, telling stories, singing, and playing games. My mom told me that her love of card games came from the many hours she spent playing them with the neighbors who were with us in the tiny shelter. We all entertained ourselves amid a vast array of people's belongings that filled the crowded space — a mix of clothes, toys, food supplies, and mattresses that literally covered every surface of the shelter floor. The crowded space did not allow us much room to move about, but somehow, having everyone close to each other offered comfort and made everything feel less scary. Sadly, not everyone had the endurance to stay in that space. A family of five that was close to ours decided they just couldn't take it anymore and tried to leave the city. Unfortunately, they didn't make it far. Their bodies were found close to the shelter.

Surprisingly, it wasn't bad all of the time. There were ceasefire periods when we were able to enjoy the surroundings of Beirut. We traveled to the ocean, where we learned to swim and enjoyed playing with turtles. We took trips up to the mountains and even enjoyed an occasional holiday party in our home. During these periods, the city would function almost as normal. Our neighborhood was made up of a couple of lower high-rise buildings, some stores, restaurants, and a huge open semi-green space where all of the kids played. It was a wonderful feeling to be able to freely run and play around our neighborhood.

However, an unspeakable, awful memory I have happened during a ceasefire period when I was able to go to school again. On my way to school, I watched, in horror, as a school bus full of children was bombed to pieces. Right in front of my eyes. I never went back to school in Lebanon after that day.

When the shelters were not even a safe place for us to be in Beirut, my family escaped to the beach and stayed in a big tent. Amazingly, the time we spent at the beach holds some of my most favorite memories of our war-torn years in Lebanon. I loved swimming in the waves and playing by the beautiful ocean. One day, I woke up super early, looked out of the tent, and saw the whole beach was packed with turtles. My heart sang as I had already realized a love for all animals at my young age. It was such a joy-filled moment for me. We had so much fun playing with them that entire day. I have no idea why the turtles all came up to the beach at the same time that day, but the images and feelings from that experience immediately surface for me when I think of my life in Lebanon. Maybe that explains why, to this day, I feel safe and secure being close to water and why I have always been drawn to living near an ocean or a lake.

# 2

# REFUGEES:
## THE MOST ADVANCED GAME OF HIDE AND SEEK, EVER!

In 1984, I was seven years old, and the war in Lebanon had been going on for nine years. By this time, my two-year older brother, David, and I had two younger sisters: Cloude, who was two years younger than me, and one-year-old Cozette. My parents, Neima and Faray, had done everything they could to keep us safe, but there didn't seem to be an end in sight to the horror that had plagued our country since 1975. It seemed that the only way we could survive was to leave. To escape Lebanon. Forever.

While in hiding, with a background of the never-ending, terrifying sounds of war, people would share stories about the welcoming country of Sweden. They would speak of Sweden as a land of peace and freedom; a place of beauty where everyone was welcome. There was talk of the kind, humane, and compassionate people who lived there. We also had relatives there whom we knew would warmly receive us. Sweden sounded idyllic — a stark contrast to living in constant fear, not knowing if we would survive another day. My parents decided that we would seek asylum in Sweden. This would be the place where we would finally live in peace.

However, reaching this land of freedom would not be easy. In fact, the journey to Sweden was one of the most distressing experiences of my first seven years, and I had experienced many by this point. My parents had saved money to secretly secure falsified documents, which were extremely dangerous to obtain, for us to be able to leave the country. The next step, and even more challenging, was escaping Lebanon on a smuggler's boat — the most advanced game of hide and seek, ever.

Crippling stress and fear gripped me as my 27-year-old mother, three siblings, and I crept onto the small boat and hid in a cramped compartment under the false cover of darkness. My father was not able to join us as he still had a responsibility to uphold with the Lebanese military, adding to my fear. He hoped he would soon be reunited with us in Sweden, but there were no guarantees.

My parents paid a lot of money for the owner of the boat to smuggle us and take us to Cyprus, where we were to then fly to Sweden. We had to remain completely still and silent while we made the 276-kilometer trip (172 miles) across the Mediterranean Sea. Any sound or movement would call attention to our presence, which meant we could be caught and sent back to the war zone, or possibly killed.

The journey to Cyprus only took a few hours, but it seemed like a lifetime. Although I was too young to fully process the gravity of the situation, I recall feeling so many tough emotions and realizing that what I felt was something no child should ever have to experience. I remember looking at my mom in that stifling space and thinking she was so brave and strong to escape a war-torn country on a smuggler's boat with her four children, no spouse, and with falsified documents. She had guts. She fought for our lives. I have always admired my mom for being such a badass woman and for doing what she did for us to survive. I must have gotten my strength and badassery from her.

After we safely reached the shore of Cyprus, we made our way to the airport, where we took the last leg of our journey to freedom. After the plane landed in our new country, the police met us and immediately took us to an interrogation facility. We were so scared. All of us kids were crying and shaking. By this point, we had destroyed the falsified passports, and we were terrified they would send us back to Lebanon. Although there were windows in the prison-like building, we were locked inside for 24 hours while we were being processed. We felt like prisoners. Finally, they accepted us as refugees and opened the doors, giving us our first taste of real freedom — we shouted for joy! I have no doubt that our crazy happy voices could have been heard from miles away. Even though the area we were allowed to be in was small, we felt free. We were FREE — in a country without bombs, without bloodshed and fear, without the need to hide for weeks on end. We had been welcomed by a country that allowed us to finally live in peace, something I had never experienced before, as I was born a child of war. Oh, what a happy feeling that was!

The trauma I experienced in Lebanon still has an effect on me today. Every time I read about or see news reports from war-torn countries or see images of children in the middle of rubble, bloody and torn, I cry my eyes out. I just can't watch that kind of news anymore. It hurts so much, as it brings up raw feelings I have from being there, experiencing the exact same thing. I am thankful that I made it out, but I still feel helpless as I feel a need to help all the children who live in war zones. I'm surprised that I wasn't more traumatized from living through a war for the first seven years of my life. I don't recall ever getting any type of therapy or emotional support. I just remember that we all had to act tough and brave, and that was that. No wonder I'm strong and resilient and have been able to take on challenge after challenge in life. And, despite them all, I have been able to thrive and have an absolutely amazing life! *Shit*, I would say, *bring it!* After all, I survived a war!

# 3

# SWEDEN:
## THE LAND OF PEACE AND SNOW

It was amazing to finally be in Sweden. It felt like a whole new world to me. Everything was different, fresh, and beautiful. I was only seven years old, but I knew that being there was a really big deal. We would finally be able to create a normal life for ourselves in a peaceful place.

After spending several days in the interrogation facility, we got on a bus and traveled two hours north of Stockholm, Sweden's capital city, to a refugee camp in the small town of Österbybruk, with a population of around 2,000. Since we arrived in the middle of winter, it was freezing cold, and there was SO MUCH SNOW! I remember riding through the countryside, watching long stretches of beautiful snow-filled forests pass by my window as we made our way to Österbybruk — another taste of freedom.

When people think of refugee camps, they usually think of areas filled with tents and no comfort or facilities. However, refugee camps were not like that at all in Sweden; they were really nice. Sweden took great care of their refugees. We were given a spacious, two-bedroom, furnished duplex in a quaint neighborhood, which was so much more than we could have ever hoped for. There were playgrounds and lots of kids to play with, all in beautiful surroundings. It was wonderful to actually enjoy being a kid, finally. There were many refugees in the camp who were also from Lebanon, so we had others "like us" to hang out with and who spoke Arabic. That helped, as we felt very different from the Swedes in the town who were all so tall and blonde and spoke a foreign language. At first, we got many suspicious looks from the locals and did not feel like we belonged, but having people there from Lebanon really helped us feel more comfortable. We now lived in a peaceful, family community where we could breathe, feel true joy for being alive, and not worry that we could be killed by bombs.

However, it was important for us to learn more about Sweden so we could feel part of our new country. We were matched with a Swedish sponsor family *(fadderfamilj)* that helped us integrate into the Swedish society. Us kids learned to speak the language and all about the Swedish way of living by playing with the kids in our sponsor family. They also helped us learn about everything else Swedish, including the culture, food, music, and much more. I wish it was still like this in Sweden and other countries that take in refugees. Unfortunately, I don't think this type of refugee camp exists anymore. I'm almost 100% sure they don't match you with a Swedish sponsor family either. I really wish they did, because it would help so many people truly feel like they belong. It would help refugees learn the language and integrate much easier into the Swedish culture and society. I believe that funding this program was well worth the investment by Sweden, as we felt we wanted to do our absolute best to make Sweden proud of us after the compassionate, terrific, and, I would say, strategically smart care we were given.

Even with all this happiness, there was still an empty spot. We missed my dad and couldn't wait for the day he could join us. We all worried about him and the fact that he was still stuck in Lebanon. I remember hearing my mom cry at night when she thought we were all sleeping. She missed him so much, and, of course, was worried about him. Finally, ten months after we arrived in Sweden, my dad was able to join us. The day he arrived was such a cheerful day! We danced and sang for days, as dancing and singing have always been my family's go-tos for celebration and happiness. Even today, dancing and singing are my go-tos when I'm down or just want an infusion of happy hormones. I've totally enjoyed getting my young son, Alex, hooked on dancing and singing as well. He's going to need an arsenal of coping mechanisms for the day when I'm not here anymore, and I want him to always feel the joy we felt when we danced and sang together. A beautiful memory of the two of us to connect to.

It is hard to describe how grateful we were that Sweden was officially our new home. I remember having a feeling of being at peace and not having to worry about hearing the crazy loud alarm warning us that bombs were coming. I didn't have to wake up, terrified and crying, because the whole building was shaking from missiles that were hitting nearby. The war had taken a big part of my childhood away, but now, in Sweden, I just had a feeling of calm. We all had a second chance at life in Sweden. This country had embraced us and captured my soul. We looked forward to creating a new life for ourselves in this wonderful, welcoming country. My parents had great lives in Lebanon before the war, but they had to leave it all behind and completely start over. Sweden gave them the gift of rebuilding their lives, and for that, my parents were so grateful. In fact, my parents had so much gratitude for all that Sweden did for us that they hung framed pictures of the Prime Minister at the time and of Swedish monarchs, King Carl XVI Gustaf and his wife, Queen Silvia, on a prominent wall in our home. Today, they live in a home with a pool that has a huge Swedish flag on the bottom. It is big and tacky, probably visible from space, but, hey, it is one way my parents wanted to show their extreme gratitude!

# 4

## HOME:
## GO BACK TO WHERE YOU CAME FROM!

With my dad now in Sweden, our family was whole again. Just two months after he returned, and a year after we landed in Sweden, we got our residence visa permits. This meant that we were now able to live wherever we wanted to live in the country. My aunt and uncle, on my dad's side, were already living in Sweden and had become Swedish citizens, so naturally we wanted to live close to them. However, we also wanted to live in a place that didn't have a lot of people from our home country so we could truly integrate into the Swedish society and not move to a mini-Lebanon somewhere else.

We decided that Lidköping would be our new home. Located on Vänern, Sweden's largest lake, this small city of about 30,000 inhabitants was very quaint, green, personal, and absolutely beautiful. Our relatives lived a one-hour drive away, so we were close enough to easily visit, which we loved, as we are very fond of our cousins.

Not to mention the fact that they were the only friends we had at the time and the only ones who truly understood where we came from and our way of living. In the years to come, we would become a very well-known family in Lidköping, the Zeitos that owned Café Elake Måns i Kopparporten.

My parents did not want to be on welfare or get any handouts, as they felt they had already been given so much, so they started working as soon as we moved to Lidköping. My dad found a job as a welder in a factory, and my mom started cleaning offices, movie theaters, car dealerships, commercial buildings, and other similar facilities. I remember helping her on the weekends and thinking what a tough job it was. The movie theaters were disgusting. I couldn't believe how people would leave all their trash behind in them. Every time I go see a movie, I remember the times I had to clean up behind people, so I make sure to throw all of my trash away when I leave. My parents also studied to learn Swedish for immigrants so they could communicate with the people of their new country. It was really difficult for my mom and dad to come to a new country without jobs or knowing the language and start their lives over again. I admire them so much and am super proud of them for all they did to give us a great life.

Since my parents worked so much and were away from the house a lot, I became the "extra mom." In our culture, it is natural for the oldest daughter to take on the role of "extra mom," but it was also necessary for me to do so in our situation. I cleaned, made sure everyone was fed, and helped take care of my younger siblings by taking them to daycare and doing anything else a parent would normally do. I had to take on a lot of responsibility very early in my life, which made me have to grow up way too fast. I don't recall ever feeling like I was a child myself.

We were among the first immigrants, non-Swedes, living in this city. Because of this, we really stood out, in both good and bad ways. Some people would find us "exotic" and interesting, while others just thought we did not belong. It was a constant struggle for us to fit in. I was bullied and beaten a lot in school for looking different and for not speaking Swedish perfectly. I remember being bullied by several classmates, but specifically one tall guy named Christian comes to mind. He always hit me and called me different racist names, repeatedly saying to me, "Go home to where you came from. You don't belong here." It was awful. I remember crying a lot when I got home, alone in my room, feeling scared to go to school. Since we were so young, I don't think they were his words, but those of his parents, who probably talked about how much they hated us being there. Unfortunately, I had to defend myself a lot and learned how to use my fists in self defense. I am not proud of doing that, but I couldn't just let them beat me. I came home many times with my eyeglasses broken in several pieces after being beaten up. I never told my parents how it happened, deciding instead to say that things just got rough while we were all playing soccer.

I loved being active and being out and about in my new town. I rode my bike everywhere I wanted to go. It didn't matter how long it took me to get somewhere, I just hopped on and went. I also had (and still do!) a great love for sports, especially soccer. Or as most of the world calls it, football. I played football a lot in school and eventually went on to play on a team. My dad didn't like that I played football, as he didn't think, at the time, that it was something girls should do. However, football really did help me feel like I fit in with the Swedes and made it easier for me to make friends. Football became my "thing" from age eleven through seventeen or so. I loved it! Eventually, my dad and I were able to share our love of football and spent many hours watching the Italian football league games. Paolo Maldini was my favorite football player. He played as a left back and central defender for A.C. Milan and the Italy national team. He is regarded as one of the greatest football players of all time, which I totally agree with, and it didn't hurt that he was extremely good-looking as well — haha. As a kid, I remember telling my dad that one day, I was going to marry Maldini!

Although we absolutely loved living in our new city and enjoyed being near a tranquil lake, life was still hard for us. We came to Sweden without anything and had to learn a new language, culture, and way of life. I think it is difficult for people to really understand just how challenging it is for adults to completely start life over and find their place in a new country.

I have always been really proud of my parents for having such a strong work ethic and being a great role model for me. My dad has always been an entrepreneur, and back then, he came up with the brilliant idea to help refugees in camps all around Sweden find the ingredients so they could cook food from their home country. He realized the ingredients they needed were hard to find in regular grocery stores. Since the import companies that sold the kind of ingredients the refugees needed were in the bigger cities, he got a license to drive a big truck, bought a truck, went to those companies, filled up his truck, and drove to the different camps, where he sold the ingredients directly from his truck to the refugees. He worked long hours, leaving early in the morning around 4:00 a.m. and coming home late at night. Eventually, he and my mom were able to open smaller stores in a couple cities where many refugees were located.

Even after my parents got to the point where they were able to have their own business and make enough money so we were able to buy a house in the suburbs of Lidköping, in a village named Vinninga, and a sailboat and travel to nice places, there were rumors in our village that my dad was selling drugs, and that was probably the reason why we were able to have all these nice things and travel. It really sucked for us kids, and I can only imagine how horrible it must have felt for my parents who worked so hard to make a good life for us.

I believe it is important for people to understand just how difficult it is, for both adults and children, to integrate into a whole new country and culture. Perhaps, take a minute to put yourself in their shoes: imagine leaving your country and all you own behind and coming to a new country to start over again. Now, imagine trying to do all that while people are not accepting you. I challenge you to think about ways you could be more understanding and even ways you could help others who are in this situation.

# CONFIDENCE
## BELIEVE IN YOURSELF ABOVE ALL

Why has confidence been an important part of my success, my journey? Why is it so important? Well, for me, confidence has been key. By believing in myself and my abilities, and just feeling comfortable with who I am overall, I've been able to take on anything life throws at me. In my professional life, knowing my worth and believing in my ability to make things happen has made people around me believe in me as well. That has definitely been a key reason for my success. When I felt confident in relationships, I felt attractive, I felt happiness, and I felt that I could be true to who I am no matter who I'm with. By not worrying so much about how I am perceived, I could enjoy and truly connect with people.

For me, being confident came organically. Perhaps it came as a result of having to work so hard to liberate myself from the Arabic culture and its typical views on women. Perhaps the more challenges I took on and thrived from, the more confident I became. It doesn't mean I haven't failed; I have, many times, but thanks to my confidence, the setbacks did not really bring me down. Instead, I accepted my weaknesses, knowing they don't change my self-worth. Even now, living with a deadly disease, confidence plays a role. I don't get worried that often, even if I probably should. My arsenal of confidence helps me cope with that too.

I believe that everyone can achieve good confidence. We all have moments we are super proud of — focus on those. Whatever made you so proud in that specific moment, use that in situations where you feel like you're doubting yourself. Nothing is really that bad. Step back and look at the situation that makes you doubt yourself: is it really that bad? Did the world go under? Nope, it most certainly did not. Scratch it, learn from it, move on. Don't get stuck in that negative spiral. Don't let it define you. What's done is done.

The more you believe in yourself and your abilities, the more successful you'll become.

# 5

# CULTURE SHOCK:
## LIVING BY THE PATRIARCHAL RULES

We remained grateful for the opportunity to create such a wonderful life for ourselves in Sweden. Sure, there were challenging times that were hard to overcome, but in the big picture, our life was great. We all loved living in Lidköping, and especially loved being close to the gorgeous lake. I have lots of beautiful and happy memories of my family spending time on the water together in our sailboat. During summer vacation, we would go out on the boat for weeks, as it had a sleeping berth. We also enjoyed traveling in Europe by car together. Every summer, we had the best time taking trips to explore neighboring countries and learning about other cultures and people. I remember feeling so excited when all seven of us, as by now my sister Teresia (who was ten years younger than me) had joined our family, would load up in our Chrysler Voyager and head out on adventures to different countries — Denmark, Germany, France, Belgium — such great memories. We were fortunate that my parents were able to build great lives again and provide us with so many wonderful things and experiences.

However, there was still a struggle between the love they showered us with and the fun times we had together versus our very conservative culture. My parents are Syrian Orthodox Christians and have always strictly adhered to their beliefs. They were raised in a patriarchal society where women are not as free, and are expected to take care of the house and children. Love relationships and having a boyfriend before you met your husband-to-be was not allowed. Men, on the other hand, are free to do anything they want. My brother was given all the freedom he wanted, which was hard for me to accept. In fact, he was even allowed to have girlfriends spend the night with him, at our house, if he wanted. Since I was now a teenager and becoming a woman, I was no longer allowed to hang out with friends outside of school. I was not allowed to go to the movies or cafés or any kind of social activities after school hours. Partying, or disco, as it was called back then, was completely forbidden for me. I spent many nights crying my eyes out, thinking about how unfair it was for me, and how much I was missing out on. It was the worst case of FOMO.

My brother could do all the things I could not. I recognized and respected that this was my parents' culture, but I didn't want it to be mine. I had already sacrificed so much of my childhood and youth to be the extra parent. That's when my long-term plan to gain my independence started. Instead of revolting and fighting with my parents, I decided I would follow their rules and not go against their cultural beliefs. I realized that I had to be very strategic in how I handled things, not only so I could eventually gain my freedom, but so I could pave the way for my sisters to be free as well. I had very factual arguments with my dad since he was mostly the strict one, while my mom just did what my dad wanted, as he was the boss. I started to make him see reason, slowly but surely. I would make him understand that by my actions of being a "good girl," I would not soil their honor, aka lose my virginity, just by having a soda with my friend after school. You see, in the end, what they were actually worried about was that I would meet someone and lose my virginity pre-wedding, and then "people," relatives or others from our culture, would see me as a "slut." To them, reputation was everything! That would literally be social suicide for them. They would lose face and be ridiculed and talked about badly in their Syrian Orthodox circles, by their peers. I had to be smart about how I eventually got my freedom, and with my parent's honor intact among their social circle of Syrian family friends. The alternative was to revolt, live a miserable life of fighting with my parents, and perhaps even lose my relationship with them forever.

Since my parents took pride in working hard and wanted to instill that in us kids, I was allowed to work after school hours. I very much enjoyed the freedom that came with working, and did that a lot as soon as I turned fifteen. I worked a variety of weekend and extra jobs just so I could make my own money. I felt a tiny bit of independence and a lot of pride from earning my own money, and I remember how excited I was to buy my first pair of Levi's. This was the start of my longing to have a successful career and live a full life on my terms!

Around the same time, I dreamed of going to the United States. I had an uncle (my mom's brother) who lived in Brooklyn, New York, so I decided that I wanted to visit him and see New York City. The summer I was fifteen, my family planned a trip to drive to Greece, Cyprus, and then visit Lebanon. I asked my parents if I could go to New York instead of going on the family vacation. Surprisingly, they let me go! Well, I had built a lot of trust with my parents by then, so that helped. I had the best time with my uncle and cousins and fell madly in love with New York City, so much so that I decided I would one day move there to study or work. It was the best experience and paved the way for planning a future in the United States.

My parents really wanted me to marry a man from our culture, even though I didn't necessarily want that. I wanted to fall in love and marry a man who would be my equal, my partner, not my boss. Someone who would love me for the independent woman I was, and not someone who wanted to change me. The summer before my senior year of high school, I was sixteen going on seventeen, and I went to Syria to stay with my grandparents and visit my aunt (my mom's sister) and other relatives. I had a lot of fun and enjoyed spending time with them. However, I had no idea, and my parents claimed they didn't either, that my aunt planned to present different eligible men for me to consider marrying. I was horrified! It was definitely an unexpected part of the trip, and, while it was part of the culture, it was not for me. After being presented with different eligible men, to whom I had to serve coffee when they visited so they could check me out, ugh, I politely declined each one. One day, my aunt and I went to visit one of her friends. While we were there, her friend presented me with two of her sons and asked me to choose which one I wanted. Seriously!? I told her that I didn't want anyone, as

I had plans to go to college and had no plans to marry. I thought this would be best so it wouldn't make her feel like I was rejecting them.

The funny (well more ironic) thing about this was that my parents had a true Romeo and Juliet love story. My mom was seventeen and living in Syria, and my dad was in the Lebanese military when they met, fell in love, and decided to be together. They fought for their love and wouldn't let anything stand in their way. One night, my mom made a rope by tying sheets together and climbed down from her window where my dad was waiting for her. They got in his car and drove all the way to Lebanon, ran away, and started their life together. Without a doubt, their love for each other was deep, and my mom was strong and tough. Shortly before she ran away, my mom's brother walked in and saw my mom holding a photo of my dad. He asked to see what she was looking at. Instead of showing him, my mom refused and put the photo in her mouth and chewed it up. Another example of my mom being brave and proof that I inherited my badassery from her! Her parents were so disappointed and mad at her that they didn't talk to her for three whole years.

# 6

# I'M FREE:
## FEMALE INDEPENDENCE AT LAST

continued to work hard, study hard, and be a "good girl" in my parents' eyes as I finished my high school years. Remember, all of this was important for me to be able to gain my independence. Traditionally in our culture, the only way for me to move from my family home would be to marry, but my goal was to go to college before I even thought about getting married. Since I had decided I wanted to study International Marketing & Business at Mälardalen University in Västerås, which was a three-hour drive from Lidköping, I would obviously need to move away from home.

When the time came for me to get my parents' permission to move and attend college, I hoped all of my efforts would finally pay off. My parents had always supported my plans to study, but it was moving away from home as an unmarried woman that was the tricky part, and unheard of in our culture. However, because I had planned and worked hard to build trust and credibility with them, I knew I had a chance. Also in my favor was the fact that my grandparents had always seen me as a good girl, and my grandpa put in a good word for me. Well, everything worked! My parents said yes! I could hardly believe it! It was a really big deal! Moving away from home to study was absolutely one of the most life-changing moments in my life, not just because I was moving away from home, which was a big event for most teenagers my age, but because I was finally gaining my independence. I was free to be a normal teenager, hang out with friends, and socialize as much as I wanted.

By far, the most fun I had in my life as a young adult was during my college years. I lived in an old hotel, called Park, that had been converted into student dorms. The eleven-floor building had twelve or thirteen rooms per floor, and on each floor, there was a shared kitchen. We all liked hanging out in the lobby where there was a large social room with televisions, pool tables, sofas, and other comfortable furniture where we could lounge around. Over 100 students lived in the building, each of us craving the opportunity to make new friends. I loved it so much! I had an absolute blast living there. I made some really great friends, some of whom are still my friends to this day. I even fell in love for the first time while I lived there. Although the guy ended up breaking my heart, I did experience what I thought was falling in love.

I have lots of fun memories of all of my friends in the dorm getting together to watch the television shows *90210* and *Friends* in the lobby. It was all so amazing. However, the fact that I was a student in another city was still a problem for some people in our culture.

Because I lived alone away from home and was not married, some people in my parents' Syrian social circles would look down on me and say that I had become "Swedified." What they meant was that I was a "loose" girl, which was absolutely appalling by the way, that they didn't have higher thoughts of Swedish women. I was once called a loose girl to my face when we were visiting with my parents' friends. And the funny thing is, I was still a virgin at that time. Thankfully, my parents defended me and told them they were really proud of me for working so hard and that I was a "good girl," whatever that means, ugh. They did not hang out with those people anymore after that. I was happy that my parents supported and defended me, but it was still hard to know that such harsh things were thought of me and even said to my face just because I lived away from home as unmarried. This belief was a huge downside in our culture, and one that I obviously did not agree with. In fact, I did everything I could to change these views when it was brought up in conversation with my parents' friends. I even was brought in to speak to classes in high schools in segregated areas and help girls and women who were having a hard time with these beliefs at home.

I did enjoy myself and partied a lot, as students do, but I also studied really hard and earned high grades. I was super ambitious and wanted to do all I could to make sure I reached the big goals I had for my future after college. I was very involved in the Student Union and Student Council, and did many other things including being a Student TV Host, Student Radio, and an organizer of different student events. Eventually, I became involved with the Business Committee that connected students with companies that were looking for talent.

I just loved being involved in everything. I soaked up knowledge wherever I could find it, and then transferred that knowledge into real action. Because of all of my focused efforts and involvement in campus activities, I was headhunted before I even finished college. This was in the late 1990s when a New Economy was first declared, as hi-tech tools and, in particular, the Internet, just started making their way into the consumer and business marketplace. Being as ambitious as I was, I totally took advantage of realizing this and started learning everything there was to learn about these new areas. Interestingly, our textbooks had not really caught up to including most of these technological developments. I ended up learning about this new industry through real-life experience when I started working in one of the first science parks in Sweden, Teknikbyn, which was located in Västerås, the same city as my university. In my last year, I studied full-time, worked full-time, and had a fun social life. Today, I can't even believe I had energy to do all that I did — like, when did I sleep!?

Two years into my college studies, I met Daniel, the man who would become my first real love, and later, my first husband. The story of how we met began while I was home from college on summer break in 1998. The regional competition of the Miss Sweden beauty pageant was to be held in my hometown that summer, and, without me knowing, one of my siblings had entered me into the competition. Someone called me at my parents' house and asked if I would come that same evening to this popular nightclub in our hometown, Stadt. Since my parents were very strict, I had never been to this nightclub before. I was super excited just to go check it out. My brother chaperoned me, which was really silly since I was living by myself as a student at the time. Once I arrived, I was asked a bunch of questions and photographed. Then they asked me to come back the following night to be part of the semi-finals. I ended up going, and I won! I went on to the Regional State Finals where I also won that competition and was crowned Miss Västergötland.

I remember my parents were so proud, as it was the first time an immigrant had won the competition. I just recall thinking it was all so silly, but it led to me spending a year participating in tons of Miss Sweden promotional activities, fashion shows, television appearances, travels, etc. There were so many obligations with my title that I had to take a break from school. I made some amazing friends during this period, and I definitely took advantage of the opportunity to have a lot of fun. I remember thinking it was ridiculous that we all had to be "on" all the time, even having to wear makeup when we came down to breakfast at the hotels we were staying in, as the cameras were constantly following us around. I actually ignored this requirement most of the time, and was probably a very annoying contestant, as I really didn't follow all the "rules" or always do what was expected of me.

During the time I was participating in the Miss Sweden events, I met Daniel Cremonini. At the time, he was a hot model from Stockholm and was represented by a major modeling agency. He had traveled all over with his modeling career, even modeling in one of the fashion capitals of the world, Italy. The Miss Sweden organization hired male models to walk us out on stage and to be part of photo shoots, etc. for the different promotional events we participated in. Well, long story short — I saw him and fell head over heels in love. I was twenty years old and thought I had felt love before with the guy who broke my heart earlier, but what I felt for Daniel was different.

After I fulfilled my obligations with the Miss Sweden organization, I returned to college, where Daniel joined me as we continued our relationship. I graduated in 2000, ready to take on the world. This time in my life was the start of so many things for me. It is where I found myself, discovered what I was good at, and grew in my confidence for what I believed I could achieve in life. This is when badass Adiba was born. I now believed that it was possible for me to achieve anything.

# 7

# MY FIRST COMPANY:
## BECOMING AN ENTREPRENEUR

After I graduated from college, Daniel and I decided to stay in Västerås so I could continue working at Teknikbyn, now Västerås Science Park. It was exciting to be working in a field I had grown to love in such a short time. One of my first projects was to organize and manage the first major tech fair at the science park, Teknikbymässan, which was a great success. I was also hired by a brilliant entrepreneur to start and manage his IT (Information Technology) team. The team consisted of college students who were studying IT and wanted to make extra money. They used their expertise to build websites for small and medium-sized companies for a fraction of the price larger companies would have charged. Remember, this was the time when the Internet was new, and people were just beginning to catch on to the idea that websites would be important for their businesses. This arrangement was a win-win since because, at the time, the only option to have a website built was by large companies that charged big money for them, which these smaller companies could not afford. The businesses we worked with were thrilled to have affordable websites, the students made money and gained valuable experience, and I loved bringing the two together.

A year after graduating, I decided that I was ready to leave Teknikbyn and the city where I had studied and move to Stockholm where Daniel was from. While we lived in Västerås, Daniel commuted back and forth to Stockholm for his modeling work, so he was happy to move back home. I have always said that Stockholm is the most beautiful city in the whole wide world and still believe it to this day. It is built on islands with bridges that connect the different city districts. We found a tiny studio on the water in the district of Kungsholmen and fell in love with it. Yet again, I found myself drawn to living in a beautiful place on the water. We bought the condo and moved in, beginning a new chapter of our lives together. This was a really big step — my formal entrance to adulthood!

I used to love taking walks along the water on Norr Mälarstrand and seeing the gorgeous panoramic views of the city. There is a Swedish song called "Stockholm i mitt Hjärta," or, in English, "Stockholm in my Heart." For me, this is what comes to mind when I think about where home is. Stockholm is in my heart, forever. Even though I was born in Beirut, grew up in a city almost five hours away from Stockholm, lived in San Francisco and now Charlotte, Stockholm will always be home and hold a fond place in my heart.

Growing up in an entrepreneurial family, it was no surprise that I started thinking about starting my own company after we moved to Stockholm. After I had taken on some smaller marketing jobs, I decided I would take the leap and start my own company. Using my own capital, I started Right Place Advertising, a company that sold ads to businesses in the beauty and fashion industry and displayed them in frames hung in restrooms at hotels, restaurants, nightclubs, airports, etc. The business was a great success! Within two years, I had signed up over 300 locations all across Sweden.

The idea for this type of business caught on in the advertising world, and after two years, I started facing fierce competition from larger companies who had bigger muscles than Right Place Advertising. Unfortunately, I ended up closing my business. Owning my own company was such a valuable experience for me in many ways. I recognized my mistakes and decided to learn from them. In the beginning, I failed to do my research and learned about my competition too late. I didn't have enough knowledge or connections in the industry I started a business in, which is super important when you start a company. I also didn't seek out advisors or other people who could have helped me build my business, as I was afraid someone would steal my idea. Looking back, I should have found a partner who had a strong network and knowledge about this industry. But, I was only in my 20s, naive, and had minimal experience in the business world.

There were, however, many positives about my experience and valuable lessons I learned by starting and running my own company that continue to serve me well. I did not have to take out any loans to get my business going, and I had no debt when I dissolved it. I also was proud of the fact that I built my company pre-social media, so I didn't have the advantage of using the Internet for free ways to

59

promote my business or putting information out there that could go viral, since that didn't exist. Back then, you had to have a big marketing budget to be seen, and I didn't have that kind of money.

Starting and running my own company was the most educational experience of my life. I learned more from starting a business than I did from the four years I spent in college. As the years went by, I became a really good startup coach, helping others to start successful growth companies that gained worldwide recognition. Today, I encourage everyone who has a dream of starting a company to go for it! Make sure to ask yourself if your business idea solves an existing problem in the market. Do you have experience and a network with connections in the industry you're addressing? If not, partner with someone who does. There is a lot of support out there for startups these days. Find people with startup experience who can support you along the way.

# 8

# THE TECH GENERATION:
## THE START OF A SUCCESSFUL CAREER

M y business office for Right Place Advertising was in a co-working space I shared with other entrepreneurs. In 2003, while I was still there, I learned about a great job opportunity from the guy who managed the co-working space. He thought I would be a perfect fit for the job, and he was right. The biggest science park in Sweden, Kista Science City, and its startup incubator, Kista Innovation & Growth (later named Stockholm Innovation & Growth, STING, now one of the largest in Europe), were looking for someone to be the Head of Marketing & Communication. After doing several intense interviews, I got the job!

Since I had the experience of working in a science park with an emphasis on the tech, innovation, and startup industries while I was in college and for a while after, this new job felt completely natural for me. I loved everything about working in the amazing world of science parks and incubators. I thrived doing all the work it took to package the various entities of a place like that, and then market them all as one brand, a brand that had an exciting and beautiful story to share with the world. My job for about five years was to do exactly that for this special place, Kista Science City (KSC).

During my time there, we accomplished so many things. KSC was going through a big transformation from Science Park to Science City when I joined. We strengthened our presence in the industry and positioned our region as a global innovation hub, which put our main owner, the City of Stockholm, on the map as an innovative hotspot. Besides my employment at KSC and the incubator, I was also hired by the City of Stockholm and the member organization, Swedish IT and Telecom Industries, to produce and lead a whole week of activities showcasing tech companies, startups, and research institutes all around Stockholm, called Sweden ICT Week. We constantly had visitors from all over the world who came to learn about our science city and how the whole ecosystem there worked. We were known globally as the "wireless valley," as we were home to many large IT and Telecom companies like Ericsson. I remember how much I loved telling visitors the story of our science city and taking them from one mind-blowing research lab or company to another. I always felt such a great sense of pride in my heart for all the amazing things that were accomplished there, and even prouder that I got to tell the world about it.

By now, I truly felt like I belonged in that world — a place where the big tech companies co-existed with the small ones; where science and innovation was everywhere. I loved working in a place where I could cross the street and hang out with researchers who were working on technologies that most people would consider science fiction, or where I could grab a coffee at a university where the next "big thing" in tech was being developed. It was pretty amazing to work in an environment that gave me a constant glimpse into the future. When people asked what I did, I would tell them that I worked "in the future." What I enjoyed most was working with brand-new tech companies, the startups. I liked listening to their ideas, sometimes really crazy ones, about how they were planning on changing a whole industry, or even the world. I enjoyed helping them navigate the startup journey they had ahead of them, all while working with the startup incubators and accelerators. I felt energized when I helped startups package their ideas into successfully branded products or solutions and then pitch them to venture capitalists and angel investors — who would then make it possible for them to grow, scale up, and take on the world.

As a young woman, it was really tough to work in the very male-dominated tech industry. I definitely had to work extra hard to make sure my ideas and the work I did got the place and attention it deserved. Many times, I had to speak up assertively in order to be acknowledged. It wasn't until I had "proven myself" and had a good track record that my work and ideas received attention. In fact, this was one of the most hardworking periods of my career. I recall many occasions when I was still at the office in the middle of the night, talking long after midnight, working away on one project after another. Luckily, I had so much fun working and such a fire for my job that it never occured to me that I could have completely burned myself out during this time. I had now made a niche for myself in the tech industry. I loved that I had discovered a great talent and passion for working with science parks and startup incubators — work that would eventually make my dreams come true.

I will always have fond memories of working with the incredible and inspiring people at Kista Science City and Stockholm Innovation & Growth (STING). People there were smart and business savvy; they were visionaries and inventors. I learned so much from the years of my career I spent there, and I had so much fun along the way. I knew without a doubt that this was the type of environment I excelled in, and I am grateful to the people I worked with who opened up this world to me.

# LOVE
## YOU KNOW, LIKE DEEP
## IN YOUR HEART KIND OF LOVE

I know it's painful, but when you actually feel real true love and allow yourself to embrace it with every fiber in your body, you can also get hurt. But, it's worth it!

The best way to truly know if you love someone or something, and I mean the kind of love that you feel not just in your heart but also in your gut and your mind, is to imagine yourself losing that love. It's really very simple. I know it sucks having to imagine losing love to know if you feel real love, but unfortunately that's how us humans work. I didn't realize how much I loved my first husband until he left me. The pain was intense. I didn't realize how much I loved my career until I got sick with a deadly disease and couldn't work anymore — I lost a piece of myself. I didn't realize how much I loved every aspect of my life, even the mundane things, until I was faced with my own mortality and the knowledge that it will be taken from me way too soon.

We live day after day taking love for granted — love for our partners in life, our family, our friends, our pets, our jobs, even for our everyday life. Do we truly love our life and the people in it? Take a minute, close your eyes, and imagine living without those people in your life, or without that job, or without the mundane things we do on an everyday basis. If you lost them, if they were not in your life anymore, how painful would that be? Do you feel the pain? If yes, that means you truly love. If no, then stop kidding yourself and move on with your life!

Love is one of the ingredients that has helped me in life — to feel the love and the pain. If the two are not there, then I haven't tried to force it. Life is too short to live without love — love makes life so much more fun! Live life, your life, the way you want it — don't just say you do.

# 9

# FIRST BIG LOVE:
## MARRYING THE MAN OF MY DREAMS

Let's go back in time a little bit. So in 2001, the same year I started my business, another big life event happened for me — I married Daniel! Daniel Cremonini was my first big love. He swept me away with his beautiful, kind eyes and his contagious smile. He gave me butterflies in my stomach and heart every time I saw him. Oh, and he was HOT! Sure, I fell for his looks, but I fell in love with both his emotional intelligence and his street smarts. I had a very fulfilling relationship with Daniel, from day one. I had not had much experience with relationships before him, but he checked all the boxes. We were madly in love, enjoyed doing the same things, and had similar views on life and the world. We clicked so well, in every way. He was a good man, smart and kind, and super charming. I felt like I was the luckiest woman on earth to have found such an amazing guy, a man I wanted to have a family with, grow old with.

Daniel and I loved living in Stockholm in our cute condo in our favorite part of Stockholm, surrounded by water. We were within

WHEN LIFE HANDS YOU CACTUSES, MAKE MARGARITAS

walking distance to everything we needed. We were so happy. It didn't matter what we did, we just enjoyed being together. Whether we were walking hand-in-hand along the water, watching one of our favorite television shows, or off exploring Stockholm, we always enjoyed spending time together.

We were a couple for almost four years before getting married. However, I didn't tell my parents about our relationship until after almost two of those years, not until after Daniel and I talked about getting engaged. They didn't know he existed for two whole years! I had not told them about our relationship before, as I was worried they wouldn't approve. Daniel was not from our Syrian Orthodox culture — his dad is Italian, and his mom Swedish. I wasn't sure how they would respond to my being with him, especially my dad. The funny thing was that Daniel had grown up in Norsborg, a segregated suburb of Stockholm where many Lebanese and Syrian people lived. Many of his friends were Lebanese and Syrian, so he knew our ways, customs, and traditions. He had gone to many Syrian parties, which was hilarious to me, as I myself had not. He actually knew more about my culture and traditions than I did.

I thought it would be best if I told my mom about Daniel first so she could help prepare my dad for the big reveal. I was going to marry the man after all, so it was definitely time. Soon after I talked to my mom, I planned a visit to see my parents. When I arrived, I asked my dad to go on a drive with me. He was always the best and most receptive to talking about things when we were driving together. So, we got in the car: he was driving, and I was in the passenger's seat. I said, "Well Dad, do you remember me telling you when I was a kid and playing football that one day I was going to marry Maldini when I grew up? Well, it turns out that I am going to marry a Cremonini!" I went on to tell my dad about Daniel and the fact that his dad was from Northern Italy, and his mom was from Sweden, and he had grown up in the suburbs in Stockholm with a lot of Lebanese and Syrian friends. It was a very big deal that I was going to marry someone who was not from our culture, religion, or national background. I was surprised, but my dad actually took the news very well. The first thing he said was that he knew I would not end up marrying someone from our culture, because I was just too independent. He said he knew that I wouldn't be told what to do, that I was too firm in my beliefs and wouldn't let a man decide things for me. He also said that it was probably for the best, and if I had married someone from our culture, I would probably be divorced within a year. I never told my parents that Daniel and I had been together for two years and had already been living together when I finally told them about him. When they visited me, they thought I lived by myself. Before they arrived, Daniel and I would go around the apartment, collecting all his stuff and hiding everything in the storage room. It was silly really, since I was a grown woman, but I did it out of respect for them.

I knew Daniel was going to propose, but I had no idea when or how. One night, we went out to an Italian restaurant we loved — Italian food has always been my favorite. After dinner, I saw dessert and champagne coming out, and then Daniel went down on one knee, in front of the whole restaurant, and proposed! I was just blown away. I had no idea he was going to do it that night! It was all so sweet and romantic. I have no idea what he said or what I said, but I do know that it was beautiful! After we were engaged, Daniel went away for three months for work. It was the longest three months.

When Daniel returned, we went on a trip to Marbella, Spain, to celebrate our engagement. This was the first time we had traveled together. Before then, it would have been too hard to explain away traveling with a man my parents didn't even know existed. I have the most beautiful memories from that trip! This was the first of many trips we took together, as we both loved to travel.

My family loved Daniel and easily welcomed him into our family. My parents even referred to him as their extra son. My siblings also grew very attached to him, especially my youngest sister, Teresia. They all saw him as another brother in the family, which made me happy that they all thought so highly of him.

So, back to 2001, which was two years after we were engaged. We got married on August 4 in a beautiful ceremony with 250 people in attendance. Syrian weddings are insane — ours was actually considered very small by comparison. By then, I was 24 and Daniel was 28. The wedding really was over the top in many ways, as it was mostly to make my parents happy. We could have easily had a much smaller and more intimate one. The Syrian Orthodox Priest who married us said things like, "and your role as a wife is to obey your husband" in the ceremony, and I remember laughing out loud and getting angry looks from the priest. You could hear my friends and sisters giggling away in the church too. However, it was a beautiful and very joyful wedding. We danced and had a blast until 4:00 a.m. Everything was perfect and a great way to start our married life together.

Daniel and I honeymooned in Playa del Carmen, a resort town in Mexico along the Yucatan Peninsula. It was amazing! I have many beautiful memories of the two weeks we spent there. Since we were both big sun worshippers, we loved laying on the beach, reading, playing cards, and soaking up the sun. We met several other honeymooners there and ended up hanging out and partying with them most every night. We really hit it off and became friends with an older couple in the group who was on their second marriage. They told the group that we should all plan on meeting back there in ten years to see who was still together, considering the 50% divorce rate. I'm not sure if anyone ever did.

I was completely swept up in our romance and the love Daniel and I shared for each other. We were truly great together, and we had a beautiful love story. I have, and will, always cherish those memories and that part of my life journey.

# 10

## MAKE A BABY:
### THE INTENSE LONGING FOR A CHILD BEGINS

A year into our marriage, I had a great job that I continued to love, and we had bought a new house in a suburban area with lots of young families that was close to both of our jobs. Our life was great, but I felt like something was missing. I was ready to have a baby.

In fact, my longing for a child was intense. Remember, I had been an "extra" mom from an early age, so being a mom came natural to me. Daniel was open to us having a baby, but he wasn't as invested in it as I was. I think he was more open to it because it was something that I really wanted. And want it, I did. I honestly have no idea why my longing for a child was, and continued to be, so strong. I just felt it in my soul, in my heart so strongly that I wanted to become a mother. I guess for some of us, the biological urge to procreate can come early in life. It also didn't mean that I was going to in any way give up on my career. I always planned to have both. At the time, I had a hormonal implant in my arm as my method of birth control, so

I made an appointment to have it removed, clearing the way for us to start trying for a baby. I remember feeling so excited the day I went to the hospital to have it removed. I thought, *Now I can get pregnant!*

We tried and tried, but each month, I would end up getting my period. This continued for many months. I was so disappointed, but I tried to be patient. I kept telling myself that I was only 25, and we had just started trying. We had plenty of time. But, I really wanted to be pregnant, more than anyone realized or could understand. Sadly, I didn't have anyone in my friend group I could share my feelings with. None of my friends were ready to start a family; most were single, so they weren't in a position to understand what I was going through. They didn't have the same longing I did. I felt so alone. It was really hard.

I so badly wanted to be pregnant that I crossed the line and became a tiny bit obsessed. I even ordered a box of 100 pregnancy tests from a company called The Stork and hid them from Daniel, because I didn't want him to know how "crazy" I was; how "over the top" I was about having a baby. I remember doing tests even before I was supposed to be able to. I looked for the smallest of signs in my body telling me that I was pregnant. At one point, I felt like my breasts were different, they were tender and had gotten larger. My abdomen distended, and I started having several symptoms of being pregnant. Even though pregnancy tests were negative, I was totally convinced that I was pregnant. I believed it so much that I had developed and was diagnosed with pseudocyesis or a phantom pregnancy. This is when the body displays symptoms of pregnancy without there being an actual fetus. This was the first of many disappointments I would experience along my path to becoming a mother.

After Daniel and I tried for over a year to get pregnant, we finally decided that we needed some help. In Sweden, you can get in line to have IVF treatments after trying unsuccessfully for a year and six months to get pregnant. Each person is given three IVF tries for free, which is a great part of the Swedish universal healthcare system. Before we could be on the waitlist, we both had to be checked. The results showed that nothing was wrong with either one of us; the doctors said there was no reason we could not get pregnant. Apparently, we were in the group of 10% of people with no explanation. That made it worse, as there was nothing we could fix!

After we got a spot on the waitlist to do IVF, we knew it could be up to a year's wait before it was our turn to have the first treatment. Daniel and I continued to try on our own to get pregnant, but I stopped being as disappointed each month when I got my period, since we were on the list for IVF. But, it was still a really emotionally tough time for me. I felt like a failure. I also didn't have anyone to talk to about it, so it was a lonely existence. Sure, it was a little easier knowing that I was on the waitlist for IVF, but I was still so focused on doing everything I possibly could to have a baby. I got online and read every single forum post out there about how to increase your chances of getting pregnant. It helped knowing there were many people online who felt the same anguish and grief over failed attempts at getting pregnant as I did. It was truly a heartbreaking and grief-filled experience to want a child so much, and then feel like a failure because you couldn't make it happen. At the same time, my career was taking off, and I was working nonstop. No, it wasn't stress that made it hard for me to get pregnant. Believe me, I asked and did try to work less. I also relaxed more for a period of time to see if that would change anything. It didn't. Soon, it would be our turn to try IVF.

# 11

# BREAST CANCER STRIKE 1:
## BUT I'M ONLY 27 YEARS OLD

In 2005, after trying my best to stay patient and positive and waiting for more than a year, we finally got the call that it was our turn to do IVF. We were so excited! The Fertility Clinic had us do bloodwork and a few other things to prepare for the process. We were so ready!

However, one thing was bothering me. I had recently felt a small lump the size of a marble in my left breast. *Surely it was nothing*, I thought. The lump grew larger, and Daniel encouraged me to get it checked out. I wasn't worried, but thought I should at least call and ask about it. I spoke with a nurse at Cityakuten, an emergency care center/clinic, and she said I shouldn't worry — I was too young to have any serious issues like breast cancer. She said hormonal changes may have caused it, and if I gave it time, it should go away. Today, I am so mad at her! Nobody should be told that they are too young and shouldn't worry. They should always have anything suspicious, any kind of lump checked out, immediately! Young people get breast cancer too, and it's a shame that mammograms are not done from a younger age!

Luckily, Daniel didn't agree with the nurse and made me go get it checked. He said to please do it for him. I'm really glad he did, because if it had just been up to me, I wouldn't have gotten it checked. I was "too busy" with my career and wouldn't have taken the time. Daniel and my sister Cozette came with me to the appointment. I had a mammogram and a biopsy of the "lump" at the same time. I wasn't concerned at all, because I really didn't think it was anything. In fact, during my appointment, several nurses and technicians repeatedly said, "You are too young for it to be breast cancer. Don't worry." Again, not OK! Not long after, I got a call letting me know that the doctor wanted to talk to me about the results. I never expected the doctor's words would be life-changing.

I took the subway, a twenty-minute ride into the city from Kista, and left my car at the office. I had planned on going to a few meetings in the city right after my appointment. I walked into the doctor's office, and he asked me to take a seat. I still wasn't worried. He then said, "We were all shocked. All of us. It is breast cancer."

I couldn't breathe. My entire world collapsed in that moment. I was devastated. I was in shock. It was as though a big hole opened, and I fell in. I was only 27. People my age did not get breast cancer, right!? They said there was not a chance this would happen. They were wrong!

The doctor told me that the tumor was small, and my breast cancer was most likely at a very early stage. He said it was easily treatable. I honestly don't remember anything he said after that. Back in 2005, there wasn't as much information about breast cancer available to the public, in other words, online. For all anyone knew, any breast cancer diagnoses meant certain death. I was overwhelmed. Shocked.

I don't remember anything about the subway ride back to my office. I do know that once I reached my office, I screamed and just collapsed — my colleagues came running to my room. It all felt so surreal. I now know that only about 5-10% of breast cancer is genetic, the rest is just bad luck. I had bad luck.

Daniel came and picked me up to take me home. I couldn't talk. I went straight to bed, where we both stayed for a long time, holding each other and just crying. At some point, Daniel went to the store and bought my favorite ice cream, Tip Top, that I munched on in bed between the crying attacks. My whole world had caved in on me. This couldn't be happening. We had just bought this perfect, newly-built house with three bedrooms, a patio, and a tiny yard. It was all so new and shiny. It was in a neighborhood we loved in Vallentuna, on the Lindö Park golf course, and with so many young families with children living there. This couldn't be happening. We were ready to be parents and bring a child into this new house, not deal with breast cancer. What was going to happen now? Was I going to die?

I scheduled an appointment with an oncologist at Karolinska Radiumhemmet who set up a treatment plan for me. Daniel went with me to the appointment. The doctor said that she recommended a lumpectomy surgery where the tumor and some surrounding tissue would be removed. It would be followed by 33 radiation treatments. After that, they wanted me to take Tamoxifen for five years to make sure I didn't get cancer again. Since I was completely clueless about breast cancer at the time, I just said, "Sure, let's do it." I didn't question any of it. She then told me that I couldn't do IVF during my treatment, because my cancer was estrogen positive, which basically meant that the cancer cells feed on estrogen and grow. When you do IVF, you are stimulated with a lot of estrogen — which would basically be a feast for my cancer. None of this was what I wanted to hear. I was supposed to be starting the process to have a baby, not getting treated for cancer. It was such a tough emotional time for me. I was so sad and cried a lot, mostly for the fact that I couldn't do IVF. I just couldn't believe it. This was not supposed to happen.

Finally, I saw the light. I couldn't stay in that dark, depressed place any longer. I got all focused and shifted my way of looking at the situation. I decided to approach my cancer treatment like it was a project, and created a project plan for my breast cancer journey. I knew how to create business and project plans really well, since it was part of my profession. I set up goals and step-by-step actions to follow. I was focused and determined. I took control.

My surgery went well. The mass was so tiny, but they also decided to take sixteen lymph nodes just to make sure the cancer hadn't spread. They all came back negative, no signs of cancer outside of the breast. It was curable, and I was totally convinced I would be clear after the lumpectomy. After I healed from the surgery, I began the 33 radiation sessions. They mapped my breast with dots to make sure the radiation was directed in the same place every treatment day. I still have those dots, as they basically are permanent tattoos. You are marked for life! I continued to work full time while I had these radiation sessions — I would have a radiation session and go right back to work. I didn't let this inconvenience slow me down or stop me from moving forward with my life. I also decided that I would take the Tamoxifen as a precaution after finishing the radiation, but only for three years instead of the five years they wanted me to take it. My plan included getting rid of the cancer and getting back on track to have a baby. I wasn't going to give up on my dream of being a mother.

My longing for a baby was still very strong, so we decided to do the next best thing — we got a puppy. We picked out our Carmen, a super cute, long-haired chihuahua and finally, when she was eight weeks home, we brought her home. Carmen became a special member of our family and brightened our days. I even brought her to work with me a lot. She loved to lay her little body next to mine, cuddled up under my sweater, and snore away without a care in the world. She was the sweetest!

My first encounter with breast cancer was indeed a shocking and emotional journey. I was grateful, though, that I had a supportive husband, family, and friends who helped me through it. I also had a very supportive boss at Kista Science City and great colleagues, which also helped a lot. The fact that I ultimately decided to approach it as a project, and broke it down with clear steps and goals to reach, helped me stay on track and away from the sadness and dark thoughts. I was not going to lose hope.

# 12

## 30 AND DIVORCED:
## WHAT JUST HAPPENED?

Two and a half years after being diagnosed with breast cancer, having surgery, going through 33 radiation treatments and taking the horrific Tamoxifen that put me into menopause, it was finally time to switch gears and focus again on having a baby. My oncologist had cleared me and let the fertility clinic know that I could now start the IVF process. I was going to turn 30 that year, so I was still very fertile when not on Tamoxifen. I was not at all worried.

We called the fertility clinic, and our journey to make a baby started. We had all the checks done so we could move forward and were approved at the beginning of 2007. With the twenty eggs and Daniel's sperm they collected, we managed to create sixteen good quality embryos. We decided we would only insert one embryo and freeze the rest. I was so proud that I had twenty eggs! I knew that there was a chance that my egg count would be lower because of my treatments, but twenty was awesome. A funny thing happened during the egg retrieval process. I recall Daniel sitting next to me, and in my foggy state, the next thing I heard was a loud thud. He had fallen flat out, fainted! Haha! I teased him a lot for it and remember telling him that he should prepare himself for the actual delivery — that would be way more gory.

The overall emotional stress of the IVF process with all the hormonal injections and numerous ultrasounds was tough. I had, however, already gone through so much that nothing could really hurt me at this point. I would have walked through fire to have a child. They inserted the embryo, and then we went home to wait. I wanted it to work so badly. I wanted to do a pregnancy test almost immediately, but my "stash" of 100 was gone! So, I waited.

The test showed negative. Not pregnant. I was heartbroken. Why didn't it work? Come on. We had done everything right. We worked with professionals, and I did everything they told me to do. We had good, healthy embryos. But now, what the hell?

I was really upset and disappointed, so I thought it would be a good idea to get away from everything for awhile. I had gone through so much emotionally, mentally, and physically, not to mention that I had continued to work long, hard hours. Even though I loved my work so much, it was still exhausting at times, especially with everything else I had been through. One of my best friends, Emma, and I decided that we would take a trip together to take a break and have fun. Daniel agreed that it was a good idea.

Emma and I went to the Greek Isles and spent a week tanning on the beach, dancing, partying, just having the best time. While we were there, I noticed that Daniel seemed to be acting weird, just by reading his texts. We had always been very loving with each other, constantly hugging and touching. People would tease us that we were so lovey dovey — we had no problem with public displays of affection. It had been "our thing" to exchange loving texts anytime we were apart, but now he didn't seem to be replying to me much at all. And when he did, something felt off. I had a nagging feeling that something wasn't right. There had been no changes in his behavior or any other signs of concern before I left, but I knew something was wrong. I just felt it in my heart.

When I got home, Daniel picked me up at the airport. Right away, I knew. I saw it in his body language and in the way he looked at me. My heart plummeted. I asked him what was going on. Even after six years of marriage and four years of being together before that, we had never had a big fight or argument. We had always gotten along so well and been affectionate with each other. Nothing would have prepared me for what he told me. He said that he didn't love me anymore and wanted a divorce. He said it wasn't anything I did or the fact that we hadn't been able to have a child, it was simply that he had fallen out of love. I asked him if there was someone else, and he told me no. He just repeated that he didn't love me anymore.

This news was another shock of my life that I never expected in a million years. Daniel and I were soulmates who were supposed to grow old together. We were so much in love and got along so well, or so I thought. It didn't make sense. At all. Fuck, one more thing to add to my misery. We were divorced on September 10, 2007. I was about to turn 30, and now I was divorced with no kids. Really, how did that happen?

Looking back, I realize that Daniel and I had grown apart and were not the same people we were when we met. We had love for each other, but we were lacking in other areas that we didn't notice at the time. We were very different people with different ambitions and drive. I was super focused on building a successful career, and wanted even more for my future. Daniel wanted more for his future too — he had dreams of becoming a psychotherapist, but just didn't have the drive to make it happen. For years, I tried to encourage him to go for it, but it wasn't until after our divorce that he actually went ahead and did it. He ended up becoming a well-established therapist, and I'm sure he is a very good one. He always had a great way with helping people navigate their emotional problems. He was a "therapist" for my siblings many times over the years. They always confided in him, and I loved that. Regardless of the way our relationship ended, I will forever be grateful for our time together. I will always cherish our beautiful memories, our love story, and forever wish him well.

# FEAR
## FEEL IT AND STILL DO IT

So I've always been called fearless, but that's not really true. Everyone has fear, everyone should have fear. Without fear, how do we feel? How do we get hurt? How do we get excited? How do we feel joy and accomplishment for conquering that fear? Fear is extremely important to feel — it helps us truly live!

However, many people let fear keep them from doing extraordinary things. Many people let the fear of failure keep them from achieving great success. By failing and getting up again, you move on to the next level in the journey of your life. You will discover parts of yourself you didn't even know existed. You will discover that you can achieve way more than you thought you were capable of. By doing the thing you fear and realizing that you survived it, whatever that thing may be, the feeling of accomplishment will be so rewarding.

I have not let fear stand in the way of living my life the way I want to. Even if I was scared, I would still go through with accepting the job that seemed super hard to do, get up on stage and talk in front of a lot of people, move to a different country where I have no friends or family, go out there and find love again, keep trying to have a child even though the fear of failure was constant, write this book and share my life with the world. The list of things I've done in my life despite feeling fear for them is long.

Dealing with the fear of dying is definitely the toughest fear I've ever had to deal with. It is super scary to carry a life-threatening disease, never really knowing where the cancer cells are more active, what part of the body is being under attack, living from scan to scan, treatment to treatment. But I'm not gonna let that fear stop me from living and enjoying the time I have left on this planet. I deal with my fear of dying by feeling it, accepting it, telling it: *I know you're there, but I don't have time for you now, I'm too busy living.* Put it in a box, close the lid, and place it far on the back of a shelf.

# 13

## 30 IS THE NEW 20:
### LIVIN' LA VIDA LOCA

I had given ten years of my young adult life to Daniel, and now we were divorced. I didn't date much before him, so it felt like I was basically starting my life over again. The moment he left, I realized that I couldn't, and probably shouldn't, plan for everything in my life. I had always been big on planning my life, even down to the smallest detail, since I was a teenager. I realized that things kept happening to me that were out of my control. My life kept changing over and over again, whether I liked it or not.

Weeks later, I remember sitting in the kitchen of the house that Daniel and I had shared and loved, paying bills. I opened the phone bill and noticed that it was much higher than usual. I looked through the list of calls to see if there was an error somewhere. Lots and lots of calls had been made to one particular cell phone number during the time I was in Greece. I checked the Yellow Pages and learned that the number belonged to one of Daniel's childhood friends, a woman that he hung out with now and then. She even visited us a few times.

I always felt like she had a thing for him, it was a special look she gave him. I remember mentioning to Daniel on one occasion that "I think she has feelings for you," but he brushed it off and said that was a crazy thought since "she's like a sister to me." So, I didn't pay any more attention to it. Clearly, that was not the case. I called Daniel right away and asked him if anything was going on between the two of them, and if she was the reason he had wanted a divorce. I repeated his words back to him, "You told me there was no one else." He said that she was just a friend, and he had needed someone to talk to. I kept pushing him, and eventually he admitted that they had started a relationship. He quickly said that they hadn't done anything together until after we had separated. Either way, it didn't matter. He had not been honest. I was so disappointed, not to mention angry! I hung up the phone and sat there, holding the phone bill. How could he have done this to me? He had lied, and that made me even more angry. I had cried my eyes out wondering what was wrong with me, why he didn't love me anymore.

After our call, I walked out on the porch, the one where Daniel and I were supposed to be enjoying a glass of wine together, not where I was supposed to be crying because he had so deeply hurt me. I realized that I could not live there anymore. It was the worst place I could be. It was pure torture to my soul. I had to move.

Then I decided — fuck it! I was not going to dwell on this anymore. Enough was enough. I was a smart, beautiful, and strong woman, and I refused to wallow in the fact that Daniel had left me. Lied to me. Betrayed me. It was not me to stay in that place. I hadn't let cancer get the best of me, and I sure as hell wasn't going to let Daniel get the best of me. I got a bottle of vodka, tipped it up, and drank straight from the bottle, something I had never done before. Then I called my sister Cozette and said, "We are going out this weekend. You and me. And we are going to party and have fun like I'm twenty again!"

That night was the beginning of a new chapter in my life. I had become a responsible adult way too fast. I had given my whole self to my marriage, a child who wasn't born, and a dream of a family that was shattered. I had survived cancer. I was ready to reclaim my young self, party, have fun, and for the first time in my life, just be reckless. I wanted to feel young, sexy, and wanted again. I was going to have as much fun as possible. We went to the most popular nightclub, where I was determined to dance with the hottest guys, just to prove to myself that I still had it. I had even rented a hotel room, being open to what the night brought. Cozette and I had a blast. We partied, danced, and fully enjoyed ourselves. I flirted and felt attractive. The whole world was a brand-new canvas for me, and I was going to fill it with fun and adventures.

I also started hanging out with my close friends more. My best friend Jessica helped me look for a new place in the city, and even helped me pack my stuff and move out of the house. She found a super cute condo on the Island Stora Essingen in my favorite, Kungsholmen. It was the first place I had bought by myself. It felt incredible and so liberating when it was time to leave the house and move away from the family-friendly neighborhood. I wasn't that person anymore — had I ever been? I continued to go out, have fun, and just enjoy time with friends. I didn't let anything hold me back. It didn't mean that when reality hit and I remembered I'd lost my soulmate that I didn't break down crying, over and over, but I kept up my "have fun agenda" and thought the pain would eventually go away. Maybe this was not what a therapist would prescribe to get over the pain, but it worked for me.

I decided to do something even more bold, just for me. I didn't want to be around for the holidays, they would be too hard to face without Daniel. Since I loved to travel, I decided to take a whole month and travel over the Holidays. Most of the time I would be alone, as my friends were spending the holidays with their families. I ended up having the absolute best experience! I went to Thailand and spent time in Bangkok, where I made some great new friends. We went out together to clubs and partied pretty hard. Since I was alone, I started talking to a group of young European men and women my first night in Bangkok. They were models and got invited to all the hottest clubs as VIPs. So naturally, I tagged along. Bangkok is not a safe place to be alone as a young woman, as I noticed the first night. The first thing I did after receiving several "propositions" was to look for people who looked safe and I could hang out with. We partied, danced, and had crazy fun. We went to different tourist sites, visited temples — I basically discovered Bangkok with complete strangers. I had never been that socially brave before, so it gave me an extra boost that I did it, traveled by myself. One of my close Swedish friends, Lotta, joined me at the end of my Bangkok stay, and we traveled to two different islands together. I went on discovering Eastern Europe, met more new friends at every stop, and had a blast with them. I am still friends with some of them on Facebook. I had never done anything like this in my life. I had the most fun, ever. I am really glad that I had these experiences. I needed to go out into the world and just have fun, to be wild and crazy and create awesome memories. I did just that for months. At the end of this time, I realized I had rediscovered myself along the way. There were parts of me that I had suppressed during my relationship with Daniel. I was a social animal and loved hanging out with a lot of people, making new friends, discovering new cultures and people. However, it was time to get more serious again. I was ready for the next chapter of my life, and was excited for the plans that had started taking shape in my head. I know, I was not supposed to plan stuff, but I couldn't help myself.

# 14

## BREAST CANCER STRIKE 2:
### THAT DIDN'T LAST LONG

I had always dreamed of going to the United States to work or study. Remember the trip I took to visit my uncle and cousins as a teenager that really locked that idea in my mind? As an International Business and Marketing major, I had planned on doing an exchange year in New York City, but decided against it because it was at the same time that I met Daniel. I didn't want to leave him for a whole year. Now that I was divorced and had no obligations, I realized nothing was holding me back. I contacted different Swedish organizations in New York and lined up several interviews. I had saved up a lot of money from all my hard work, and decided I would invest it in getting immersed into the American business culture. I signed up to take a six-month business executive course in Boston, Massachusetts. I sent in my application and was accepted. The course would start in April, so I had a couple of months to make all the necessary arrangements.

In January of 2008, I resigned from my job and had to give a three-month notice before I could leave. This gave me time to finish up all I had to do in Sweden, and make sure everything was lined up in the U.S. I also had to get health insurance in the U.S, which I did through the Global Travel Agency. As part of the process to get insurance, I had to get a full physical, which included a mammogram, since I was a breast cancer survivor. I didn't think anything of having to do this, because I knew I had gotten rid of all the evil cancer. I mean it was very early stage, one small tumor, and they said they got it all.

Also during this time, I wanted to get some dating experience, so I created a profile on Match.com and ended up going out on a few dates. I just wanted to have some fun while waiting to "move" to the U.S. I connected with a guy named Magnus who seemed nice, funny, and adventurous. He looked like Clark Kent, Superman, in his profile picture. He was a geeky tech engineer who also had a passion for kitesurfing. Perfect! I love superheroes, tech, and going on adventures, so Magnus was a perfect match for me. We chatted for a while and decided to meet up. We met at a café in Gamla Stan, hit it off, and went on two more dates that week. This was the first week of February. I wasn't looking for anything serious since I was leaving, but it was fun to go out and date again.

February 8, 2008 is a date I will never forget. It was significant for two reasons. The first reason — it was the day I went to the doctor to get the results of my mammogram. I couldn't believe what the doctor told me. It happened again — I had a recurrence! Seriously!!! Breast cancer, strike 2! Why was this happening to me again? My breast cancer had returned in my left breast at the site of my lumpectomy scar. There were two new, very small tumors. The doctor said the surgeon had not taken enough breast tissue to get margins during the lumpectomy surgery, so over the last three years, the remaining cancer cells had grown into two new tumors. The doctor assured me that everything would be OK, because they found it early. Well, that's what they said the first time.

The second reason this day was significant had to do with my colleague and friend, Jocke. A 31-year-old man, Jocke had been diagnosed with breast cancer sometime before I was diagnosed the first time. Yes, men do get breast cancer too since they also have breast tissue. He and I grew close as we shared this journey together, understanding the horrible journey it was. More so for him, as his breast cancer had spread by the time doctors took him seriously. Although he found the lump early and told doctors about it then, he had to get to deadly stage 4, metastatic breast cancer, to finally be taken seriously. By then, it was too late. I watched him get sicker and sicker every day at the office since he kept working until the end of his life. The day I went to the hospital and received my second diagnosis, Jocke was also in the hospital, taking his last breath. He died from metastatic breast cancer. I didn't know he had died until a week later. My work friends wanted to spare me since I had just gotten my own cancer news. It made me super sad to hear that I had lost my friend to this horrific disease, and on top of being diagnosed again with breast cancer. His funeral ceremony was beautiful and so, so sad. I cried my eyes out for him, and for me, since everything was happening at the same time. I also completely broke down in the parking lot after the funeral. I recall having survivor's guilt for many years after. I will never forget him or the close connection we shared. Now that I have metastatic breast cancer myself, I can truly understand the struggles he went through. RIP, Jocke.

Now I had this new, early stage breast cancer diagnosis that didn't at all fit into my plans of moving to the U.S. Alright, so what now? The tumors were tiny, but they were still cancer. Yet again, my life story was changing. I thought I had completely moved on from tough challenges, but I was going to have to go through it again.

I remember feeling helpless at first. I wondered why this kept happening to me, but I also felt empowered with the thought that I could handle this. This time I felt more prepared. I had the tools. After the initial shock faded, I realized I knew how to deal with it. I was so angry that cancer was interfering with my plans yet again. The bright side — I wasn't dying, and the U.S. would still be there when I was done with treatment.

The doctors recommended that I have a mastectomy and the highest dose of chemotherapy for eight months. They wanted to treat it more aggressively this time to make sure it went away forever.

This experience helped me realize that I had more strength within me than I realized. The truth is, I believe we all do. We just don't realize how strong we are until we are faced with something that is very challenging. Strength rarely comes from pleasure or an easy life, it comes from hardship and pain. I have faced many obstacles throughout my life, beginning at a very young age. Each time, I somehow found the inner strength to move forward. Sometimes I had to dig deep, but I always found it and held on tight when I did.

I've always believed I have so much to live for, and I still do. The only thing that will make me let go of that strength is death itself.

# 15

# SECOND BIG LOVE:
## MY KNIGHT IN SHINING ARMOR

I was determined to face this second breast cancer diagnosis head on. I knew what I was in for, and I had my own tools to deal with it. I immediately called on all my knowledge from my previous breast cancer experience and all the research I had done. I developed a plan that essentially made this round of cancer into a one-year project. One year, that's all it was going to get from me. I was more in control this time, but my family and friends were not. They didn't have all the knowledge I did. They didn't know the detailed plan for how I was going to be done with cancer, once and for all. They were devastated by my diagnosis and felt completely lost. While they were worrying and crying, I was focused on staying on the path to complete each step of my plan. It actually felt weird to me that I was the one who was the least worried. Since I had gone through all of this before, I knew that knowledge was power. The knowledge I now had made it easier for me to deal with the cancer and helped me focus on what needed to be done. Most importantly,

I knew that this was not going to kill me. I could do this. I decided to let everyone know what I knew, and let them in on my project plan, "eradicate cancer."

Thankfully, I had not left my job yet, I had just resigned, so I just un-resigned and was then eligible for paid sick leave. With the sick leave benefits and the money I had saved, I knew I would be OK financially.

During all this turbulent time, I had a personal issue to take care of. I had gone out on a couple of dates with Magnus, and while we enjoyed each other's company, I had to tell him that this was where it ended. It was not because I didn't want to see him anymore, but I didn't want him to feel obligated to date me out of pity. I mean, we hardly knew each other. We went out to dinner, and I told him that I had recently received bad news and I wasn't sure that it made sense for me to date right now. I told him about my cancer and that my reality was not going to be pretty for the next year. I offered him a "free pass" from feeling any guilt if we didn't date anymore. I added that I would lose my hair and breast and be sick a lot — none of that was your typical early dating material. Magnus's response completely surprised me. Eh, wow! He said that he liked dating me even if it had only been a couple times, and he felt a deeper connection with me. He wanted to keep dating and see what happened. He said he had no problems with being there with me as I went through all this. Wow! I was totally floored. I didn't expect him to respond this way at all. He was a super nice guy and seemed like a lot of fun. I had also felt that deeper connection, so if he was up for going on this journey with me, that was fine with me! This handsome, adventure-loving, crazy smart guy who was lots of fun and cracked jokes laced with "nerd humor" had now joined forces with me on the path to kick cancer's ass.

My attraction and feelings for Magnus grew. He gave me butterflies, making it possible for me to fall in love again. Little did I know that Magnus would become my Knight in Shining Armor through this whole endeavor. Or maybe I should call him "My Romantic Comedy Hero." There was a lot of romance; he made me laugh a whole lot in his own nerdy way, and our relationship was one big adventure.

Magnus went to many doctors' appointments with me and asked a lot of questions. He paid close attention, did a lot of research, and took so many notes. He was such a knowledge nerd, and because of him, I learned even more about breast cancer and treating it. Our relationship grew very close in a short time, because he was involved in an intimate part of my life, which I really didn't mind. He helped me keep a good, positive attitude about everything.

We had only dated a few weeks when Magnus suggested that we go on a trip together before I had my mastectomy. He was into kitesurfing, so he suggested that we go to Venezuela to a beautiful kitesurfer's paradise. In April of 2008, Magnus and I went to Venezuela and stayed in a bungalow on a beautiful, sandy beach along turquoise, crystal clear water. We escaped into another world filled with beautiful music, super tasty food, and romance. We had an incredible week, and we both felt it — we were falling in love. In fact, Magnus asked me if I wanted to "go steady" with him, haha! It was so cute. I will always be thankful for that week, for the great sense of adventure we had in common, and for the tremendous joy and love for life we shared. I have the best memories of that time, despite the challenges that awaited me. Magnus was a huge gift in my life, such a contrast to all that I had going on. I will always be grateful for my Knight in Shining Armor.

The night before my mastectomy, I decided that I needed to remove the drama and relieve the worry my loved ones had about my upcoming surgery and formally say goodbye to my breast. So I invited fifteen or so people — my mom, sisters, and my girlfriends — to my condo for a Farewell Boob Party. We had a breast theme with a breast cake and breast cards, we told breast jokes, enjoyed music and dancing, opened breast gifts, and had a "thank you for long and great service" ceremony for my breast. Oh, and there were bras everywhere as I had told everyone to wear a bra on the outside of their shirts. Bras were worn in the most creative ways, from hats to suspenders. It was hysterical! I was in a good place and knew that life was good even though I was going through something so tough.

I am so glad we went on the trip and had so much fun before my surgery, and that I had my breast party, because the recovery after a mastectomy is a long and painful one. So much pain. I did reconstruction at the same time as my mastectomy, which meant my body had a lot of healing to do. However, I realized too late that I should have put more thought into picking out a new breast. They were, thankfully, able to save my skin and nipple and use it as part of my reconstruction. Unfortunately, I ended up with a breast that was hard as hell and very tiny, as I was very skinny at the time. I chose a breast size that reflected the size I was at the time. Over time, the breast sunk in and became less and less visible. My other breast changed as my body changed, as I gained weight, had periods or experienced any other hormonal changes. This meant that my natural breast grew, and it continued looking larger than my reconstructed breast, making me lopsided. I always encourage women to think hard about what kind of breasts they want after a mastectomy and encourage them to talk to experts and think about what their future self might look like. It really makes much more of a difference than people realize. Some people even choose to skip the reconstruction all together, and I can totally understand that.

I felt sad about losing part of my femininity when my real breast was gone. There was no sensation. It was a dead and hard thing that affected me more than I thought it would. I guess it made the cancer more tangible. Back in 2008, people didn't really talk about this part of breast cancer, but it is a bigger deal than people think. It is talked about much more today thanks to social media. I had to find a way to cope with the grief I had for losing my breast, so my oncologist referred me to a therapist. I only went once, because the therapist didn't "get me." This person ended up making me more depressed. Thankfully, I was able to dig into my tools and find a way to cope. Therapy can be very helpful, it just didn't work for me at the time. I was also still riding high on some love endorphins, which helped me through my recovery.

Before I started chemo and only three months after Magnus and I started dating, I realized that I needed to harvest eggs, since the chemo would make me sterile. The fertility doctor said that I would have the best chance of becoming pregnant in the future if I had embryos, meaning eggs that had been fertilized with sperm. Ideally, they wanted me to freeze both eggs and embryos. All of this had to happen right away, as I was in the most fertile part of my menstrual cycle, and they didn't want to delay starting my chemo. I was sent home with needles and the hormones to inject, the whole kit. I was shooting injections into my abdomen to stimulate my ovaries that same afternoon my friend, Emma, was at my place. I told her all about this whole ordeal while I was injecting myself. All my friends knew how important it was to me to be able to have children in the future. My longing to become a mother was always there in the background, and it hurt every time I thought about all the failed tries. I told her what the doctor had said, and how I realized that I had to ask Magnus, a guy I had only dated for three months, if he would like to fertilize my eggs. That this might be the only chance we had to have our own biological children sometime in the future. I didn't think he would, I mean we were not "there" in our relationship yet, far from it, but it didn't hurt to ask.

As I shared this with Emma while injecting myself with hormones, we both looked out of the window and saw Magnus parking in my driveway. If I was going to ask Magnus, now was the time. Emma wished me luck and left. Magnus talked to Emma for a bit as she left, and he headed inside. I was super nervous, but I wasted no time and got right to the point when he walked through the door. "So, I could be sterile after chemo, and I'm doing these injections to help me produce eggs. If you and I are together in the future and decide to have kids, this could be our only chance to have our own. So, I was wondering if you would be interested in fertilizing my eggs." He immediately said, "Yeah of course! Where do I give my sperm?"

Wow! I loved him for that! Who does that without hesitation!? His response that day meant more to me than he realized.

The next day we were at the fertility clinic where Magnus had to answer a lot of questions before he could donate his sperm. The fertility clinic had to make sure that he was mentally stable and OK to do the procedure in the first place, and that I hadn't forced him into it, since they knew we had not been a couple for that long. It was all just so surreal. They also had to make sure he had good-quality sperm. Well, his sperm count was very high, and the quality was great. I remember him playfully repeating his sperm count aloud, "350 million!" Both of these points made Magnus super proud. His incredible attitude meant so much to me. I ended up freezing both embryos and some eggs at the same clinic where I already had embryos stored from my IVF experience with Daniel. In Sweden, they save your frozen embryos for five years, free of charge. Before they discard them, they send a letter asking whether or not you want to keep them frozen. Daniel's and my embryos were only a year old and still in the freezer. So now I had two sets of frozen embryos from two different men, and no baby. Of course, years later when it was time to discard the embryos I had with Daniel, the fertility clinic mixed them up and accidentally discarded the ones I had with Magnus. When I received the lost reminder letter and realized what had happened, I was glad that by then I was no longer with Magnus, and those embryos were not going to be used. I would have probably sued the clinic if that had not been the case.

# 16

## CHEMO SUCKS:
### LET'S MAKE IT FUN

Without a doubt, recovery from a mastectomy sucked, but chemo sucked even more. The oncologist gave me a really nasty chemo called FEC, a combination of three chemo drugs that are commonly used in treating early stage breast cancer. It made me so sick, but I was determined to knock the cancer out. I had treatments every three weeks for eight months. The first week after chemo was the worst. I had a lot of nausea. They gave me anti-nausea medicine that helped a little bit. Mostly I felt like I needed to vomit but couldn't. It was a horrible feeling. Everything I ate tasted like metal, and I had a constant metal taste in my mouth. So gross. And I was very fatigued, didn't have any energy at all the first week after treatment. I also didn't want anyone around at all during that week, not even Magnus. The second week, I felt better and got out of bed more but still wasn't keen on having too many visitors. My mom could not stop crying when she saw me, which made it harder for me. At the same time, I knew it was devastating for her and my dad to see their daughter so sick. The third week, I felt much better and decided that I had to add some fun to the misery I was experiencing. I decided I would plan fun adventures on that week every month.

Magnus's wonderful parents had a house on the ocean in Gävle, facing the Baltic Sea, so we went there a lot after my surgery and during the third weeks of my chemo treatments if we weren't off on a big adventure. It was beautiful there, and so calming, especially during the first few months of my treatments since it was summer in Sweden. I loved spending time at their house that was surrounded by nature. I would take long walks in the forest with my dog Carmen, go rollerblading on the empty winding roads, go swimming, or just lay on the boat deck. Magnus' parents are wonderful people who made sure I was comfortable, and we had a great time when we were there. His dad told the most fun stories, also in a nerdy way, so I could totally see who Magnus got it from. We had our own guest house on the lot, so we had a lot of privacy, so I could decide whether or not I wanted to hang out.

One morning after I had two or three chemo treatments behind me, I woke up and noticed huge chunks of hair on my pillow. And my scalp was in pain. No one had told me that it was physically painful to lose your hair during chemo. It literally feels like each hair is being pulled out of your head by the root. It is awful. I told Magnus it was time to remove my hair and asked if he could shave it off for me. Losing my hair was a really tough thing for me, as I had always had very long, thick and lustrous hair, a trademark for Middle Eastern women. It was hard to let it go. Magnus made it as fun and light of an event as he could. He even set up a camera on a tripod and filmed the whole thing. He helped make a really difficult part of this journey a little better. I cried and laughed intermittently while my hair was falling down to the ground.

I had already had an appointment with a wig maker, and a wig was ready for me to wear when the time came for me to need one. This was the beginning of the complicated and expensive relationship between me and my hair. In Sweden, you are given a stipend as part of your cancer care to purchase wigs and false eyelashes. It wasn't much money, basically enough to cover the cost of one or two wigs. That money was used up quickly, though, and I paid much more out-of-pocket as I ended up buying all kinds of wigs in different shapes and colors; some for professional use and some just for crazy fun, like the ones in pink. To lighten the mood about losing my hair and help remove some of the drama, I decided to have a wig party at my place. Magnus helped me organize it. We invited all my friends and some of his and made it a requirement that everyone wear a wig. Between our friends' wigs and my own, there were so many really creative wigs, in all shapes and colors. I gave an award for the most creative wig, which my friend Ida took home for being an Amy Winehouse lookalike in hers. We had one hell of a party!

Wigs continued to be a big deal to me. In August of 2008, I went to New York to attend my cousin Christine's wedding. I remember that I wasn't happy with the wig I brought with me, so I decided to schedule an appointment at the wig store where Tyra Banks bought her wigs so I could buy one for myself. That was the most expensive wig I had purchased by far! I got lost on the subway, which made me late to my wig appointment, making me late to the wedding on Staten Island. Let's just say I put way too much focus on my hair and now think about how much money I could have saved, not to mention the annoyance and wasted energy I had put on my hair.

During one of the "third week" periods, we went to Varberg. I was attending a week-long kitesurfing class. I was really excited, as Magnus had already taught me bits and pieces, so I felt I could do this. We lived in a house with other people who were also attending the kitesurfing class. It was so much fun! We didn't know anyone at the beginning of the week, but after living with them and attending class together, we became close. I tried to hide the fact that I was wearing a wig, as I didn't want everyone to start pitying me, only that didn't go as I had hoped. Let's just say that wigs and kitesurfing don't mix well. It was a lot of fun, and I'm glad I tried it, but it wasn't really my sport. I was more of a football (soccer) girl.

Another "third week" adventure Magnus and I went on was in Amsterdam. We stayed in the coolest boutique hotel, where each room was like a piece of art. We biked around, enjoyed boat rides in the canals, ate great food, and had so much fun. As the saying goes, "when in Amsterdam..." Yes, I did what many others did in Amsterdam: I smoked pot. However, I was such a rookie, as I had never smoked pot before. We went to a "coffee shop" where I just took a few puffs, but had the worst reaction (trip) to it. First of all, the pot was way too strong for someone who had never had it before, plus I was on chemo, so I'm sure it was pretty stupid of me to do it in the first place, not knowing how my body would react. I remember thinking all the bikes I saw were monsters that were chasing me, and that the police were searching for me to put me in jail, so I tried to hide everywhere. I thought Magnus was saying mean things to me when he was in fact trying to calm me down and take care of me. I got very sick and threw up everywhere. I was a mess! The worst part about it was that I thought I was blind. I couldn't see anything. Of course I couldn't, I had my eyes closed! Needless to say, pot doesn't mix well with me. I must be allergic or something, as I tried it for cancer pain management and insomnia a decade later as a stage 4 patient. It messed me up again, so I gave up on it.

Magnus helped make a really tough time in my life so much better in many ways. I can't thank him enough for all he did for me. I will always be grateful for all the laughs, adventures, and fun times I had with him, and for his love, care, and kindness. He is such a special man. Thank you, Magnus!

# CHANGE
## LIVING LIFE TO THE FULLEST
## IS ALL YOU CAN REALLY PLAN FOR

Change is inevitable. The only thing you can really plan for is embracing whatever life throws at you and making it into wonderful chapters of your life. I was a super planner. In my early twenties, I thought I could plan my whole life, every step, every event, the whole journey… married life, children, career. Then, at age 27, in the midst of my career and trying to start a family with my first husband, everything changed. I was diagnosed with breast cancer. Strike one. My early-stage, stage 1 cancer was treated, my career and married life continued, but our desire to have a child remained unfulfilled. After ten years of being with the man I thought I would grow old with, we divorced. I had not planned on being divorced at age 30 with no children, but that very big change in my life closed one chapter only to pave the way for many wonderful and exciting chapters ahead.

Change made my dream of working and living in the U.S. come true. It opened up a great opportunity for my career. I traveled the world and met a lot of new and wonderful people who became lifelong friends. I fell in love again, and after many years of longing for a child, I finally had my baby boy. I have experienced events that turned out to be exciting and exhilarating. All things I did not initially plan for. I learned to not take things that happen too seriously and to enjoy the struggles, because with them came exciting changes. Instead of expecting life to go as planned, I expected change and decided to embrace it and make one hell of a life out of it. Even now that I'm living with a terminal disease, I try not to plan my life too much, 'cause who knows what tomorrow will bring.

# 17

## BORED:
## LET'S START A COMPANY

In September of 2008, I was bored from not being intellectually stimulated. My cancer treatments were going to be finished in November, and I had already technically resigned from my job, so I wondered what I was going to do next. Hey, why don't I start a company? With the experience and knowledge I had in the tech, innovation, and startup industry, I founded a business called Startup Communication. Our tag line was "Branding you from the start." My goal was to help startups in the tech industry all across Sweden with their branding, so they could position themselves in the international marketplace. I had helped brand the startups we coached at STING, but I was ready to do the same thing on a larger scale. I started writing a business plan while I was in bed, sick from chemo. Because of my breast cancer, I decided that I would use pink as one of the three colors in my logo. I even started scheduling meetings with incubators and accelerators in several cities in Sweden for right after my last chemo appointment. I had a lot of connections in the industry, as I had worked in it for almost a decade by now. As soon as I finished my treatments, I would be ready to go. I also signed up for some executive courses at Berghs School of Communication, a highly esteemed school in branding, communication, and PR to refresh my own knowledge.

Said and done. I launched my business in November, and soon thereafter, word quickly spread, and I had several clients lined up. In some cases, I was also offered the opportunity to be part of the coaching team at a few incubators as a steady gig. All of the work I did went through my company, as I did not want to be an employee again. I wanted to always be free to decide what projects to take on or not. I loved the fact that I could now work with innovative companies all across Sweden. I even coached startups at the science park, where everything started for me a decade earlier in Västerås. It was incredible to learn about all these creative innovative startups that were housed all over the country — from small towns in the North to larger cities in the South — Sweden had incredible innovation everywhere! I traveled all over the country visiting incubators and exploring the ecosystems and coaching startups. I loved my work and also appreciated that I was able to generate income again.

In the spring of 2009, I drafted an idea to pitch to the Swedish Institute, a government agency under the Swedish Foreign Ministry. One of their many tasks is to spread information about Sweden outside of the country. In other words, they were in charge of Sweden as a brand. In my business, I kept running into amazing, creative, and brilliant innovations that I realized the rest of the world did not know about. I decided it was time that changed, and

I was just the person to make that happen. You see, every country is also a brand, and just like any brand, it is measured and ranked every year based on its reputation globally. It's sometimes also called place branding. A lot of work goes into branding a nation to make sure that people's perception of that country is what you aim for it to be. It helps draw visitors, companies, investments, and talent to the country. It also helps with international relations with regard to different political issues.

I met with the branding manager for Sweden at the Swedish Institute and shared my idea with him. Sweden has always been known to the rest of the world as being a liberal, green, and neutral democracy. We are known to excel in design, music, and fashion. What the world didn't know was that so many innovative ideas and companies had originated in Sweden and were made in Sweden. The Swedish society has long fostered innovation and entrepreneurship. When it comes to research and development (R&D), Sweden invests, as a rule, more than 3% of the country's growth domestic product (GDP) in R&D. This is more of an investment than many other countries make. Green technology and life sciences are two fields in which Swedish researchers and companies excel. Sweden is also a leader in wireless and telecommunication. A well-functioning infrastructure has always been vital to Sweden's development, as the country is large, stretching far from north to south. Policies offering easy access to technology and the Internet have contributed to making Sweden the innovative nation it is today. For example, in the 1990s, the Swedish government pushed out a widely developed broadband network and Swedes' early access to fast Internet coupled with subsidised computer-lending programs helped cultivate a society of early adopters. We are a small country with big ideas! Considering that Swedes only represent 0.13% of the global population, it is pretty incredible that we always get very high rankings in innovation surveys, like the Global Innovation Index, and are continually ranked as one of the most competitive countries in the world by The World Economic Forum (WEF). I bet you didn't know that IKEA, H&M, Ericsson, Skype, and Spotify, to name a few, are all Swedish companies. The super annoying game, Candy Crush, was created by the Swedish company, King, and the popular game, Minecraft, is Swedish. Inventions like the telephone handset, computer mouse, Tetra Pak, adjustable wrench, the pacemaker, dynamite, GPS, the technology behind flat-screen monitors, safety matches, the three-point seatbelt, the zipper, the walker, and so many more things all came from this super tiny country with a population that is less than that of Los Angeles County. Even the famous Coke bottle was designed by a Swede. OK, I think you get the picture.

I pitched my idea for a pop-up road show called "Innovative Sweden" that would display the great innovations from Sweden in other countries through workshops, programs, and a mobile display showcasing brand-new innovations from Swedish startups. This idea was huge and would involve many departments within the government of Sweden if it were to actually work. I pitched my idea, using the detailed slides I had prepared, to a room with ten people who had different roles within the Swedish Institute. I didn't hear back for a very long time. When they finally did get in touch with me, they said they were still talking to different people about my idea, and would get back to me if there was an interest in moving forward with the project.

In the beginning of 2010, things seemed to be positively moving forward in my life with regard to my career. However, my personal life was a different story. I realized that I had come to a crossroads with Magnus and had to make a really difficult decision about our relationship. He had always been great to me in every way, but if I stopped and really thought about whether or not I was in love with him and if he was the one for me, the honest answer was no. We had moved in together very early in our relationship and now lived in a beautiful 1920s condo we purchased together, also on Kungsholmen, for the last one and a half years. Magnus had indicated several times that he wanted more from our relationship. I had a feeling he was going to propose any time now, and I really wanted to make sure I knew what I wanted before that happened. Sadly, I realized that I was in love with our love story more than anything else.

I really appreciated everything Magnus did for and with me during a really tough time in my life, which made it even harder to come to this decision. I wanted to be true to myself and to him. I knew I was going to break his heart. It broke my heart into a million pieces to say goodbye to him. It was truly one of the hardest things I've ever had to do. I will forever cherish the two wonderful years of life I had with this wonderful man. Today, he is now a proud dad to two little ones, and I am so happy for him.

By the spring of 2010, my business had grown, and I was working with many clients, including Stockholm University Innovation, SU Innovation. They asked me if I wanted to be part of a study tour group to go to Silicon Valley in the U.S. that May. *The U.S., SILICON VALLEY, OH MY GOD, YES!!!* In the Swedish tech and innovation industry, we had always looked up to this global innovation hotspot — Silicon Valley. Established benchmarks with it. Now I had a chance to go for one week and learn about the Silicon Valley ecosystem and meet many inspirational people. I was so excited — like a kid at Christmas!

I traveled a day ahead of the study group so I could visit San Francisco and explore the area. As soon as I arrived at my hotel room and looked out of the window onto Union Square, I felt like I had come home. Even though I had always said I wanted to live in New York, right away I just had this feeling that I belonged in San Francisco. When my colleagues arrived, I told them, "So I've decided, I'm going to move here within a year." They probably thought I was kidding (I moved to San Francisco ten months after). We had such an incredible week! We met a lot of super inspirational and interesting people, and learned so much about the whole ecosystem — from large tech companies like Google to universities like Stanford and Berkeley to incubators and accelerators. We met with venture capital representatives and angel investors. I was in heaven, and absolutely fell in love with San Francisco and Silicon Valley. I loved everything about it. While I was there, I also noticed that Sweden was pretty invisible in Silicon Valley — a possible opportunity for Sweden and me. I wanted to investigate further.

# 18

## USA TAKE 3:
### FULFILLING THE AMERICAN DREAM

I decided it would be a good idea to explore Silicon Valley and some other places in the U.S. even more, so I made plans to go back for three months on my own dime. During this three-month period, I planned to also visit the Swedish consulate in Los Angeles, the Swedish Embassy in Washington, D.C., and meet with people at the Swedish American Chamber of Commerce in San Diego. My goal was to figure out how I could position Sweden in Silicon Valley as a country with great innovative tech ideas and startups, to essentially promote Sweden as a valuable resource and investment opportunity in the tech and innovation industry. No organization had given me this assignment, I just wanted to do it. Since I had my own company, and it was summer vacation time in Sweden, I could allocate the time and money to make it happen.

When I arrived in early July, I hit the ground running and never stopped. I visited all the Swedish organizations mentioned earlier. I also met with incredible people at most of the co-working spaces, incubators, accelerators, universities, research institutes, VC firms, and as many tech companies as I could get access to. If there was a connection to be made in this area, I tried to make it. I managed to create a great network and learned a lot about how Sweden and Swedish tech and innovation was perceived or not perceived at all. I was high on inspiration I had gotten from all the incredible companies and people I had met, and was even more convinced that I belonged in this place of visionaries and doers. In September of 2010, just a week before I planned to go back to Sweden, I got a very important call. The Swedish Institute was now ready to go ahead and move forward with the project "Innovative Sweden" that I had pitched almost a year and a half earlier. It had taken them that long to get every agency and person needed for the project on board. That is Swedish bureaucracy for you, consensus is key. I couldn't believe it! I was thrilled! I would be realizing a vision I had — to put Sweden on the world map as an innovative country. Yay! They, of course, wanted me to get started on the project right away.

As soon as I returned to Sweden from the U.S., I started working. We assembled a core team of people needed to put all the pieces of the project together. I mentioned my discovery from the research tour I had done in Silicon Valley that Sweden was pretty invisible in Silicon Valley. I suggested early on that this area would be the best place to launch the Innovative Sweden road show, the first stop on the world tour. They eventually agreed! The Swedish Institute arranged for me to apply for a Diplomat Visa, as I would be working as a consultant for the Swedish Government. Woo Hoo! I was finally moving to the U.S. — realizing a long-held dream. A dream I had since I was twenty, and I was now 34. Third time's the charm, as they say. I was so excited, I could hardly stand it.

I had a lot of fun scouting all of Sweden for the innovative startups we were going to include in the roadshow. Planning and packaging this whole project with the talented people at the Swedish Institute was a very rewarding task. Since I wasn't an employee but a consultant, I could come up with all kinds of crazy ideas. I also didn't hesitate to voice my opinions on how I thought things needed to happen in order for us to be successful. Companies all over Sweden applied to be a part of the program since we had been able to generate so much national interest. We had a selection committee that worked hard to select the top innovative startups that would be presented as part of the story and the showcase. We also had to determine which countries we would visit after the U.S. and how to work with the other country representatives. This work called for a lot of diplomacy and coordination with people in many countries. It was nonstop work around the clock, and I loved every moment of it!

I traveled back to the U.S. during the end of December 2010 for a couple of weeks so I could prepare and plan for my move there. My youngest sister Tess was going to start attending Santa Monica College in the winter of 2010, so I was also there to help her get settled in and make sure she was in a safe area of Los Angeles. Being ten years younger than me, she always looked up to me as someone to turn to for support and advice. Since she was born, I have been like an extra parent to her, and have always wanted to make sure she was safe and in a good place. Big sister syndrome.

I was so excited I would be living close to her in the U.S. Just having family close by meant a lot to me. We went to Las Vegas on New Year's Eve and brought in the new year together — what a crazy fun time! Then I drove from Las Vegas to San Francisco so I could figure out where I wanted to live and reconnect with people there. Since I was going to be living there, I needed to start laying the groundwork.

After Magnus and I broke up, I sold my part of the condo to him and bought my own place in the same area. It was a fixer-upper that I completely renovated and decorated in my own style. I loved it but, as luck would have it, when I was completely finished with it, I found out I was going to the U.S. I planned on going there temporarily, a year to start, to try it out. Even so, I decided to sell my condo and everything in it, since the housing market was hot, and I had made a big investment in renovating it. I only kept enough personal items to fit into three suitcases. I saved a few personal mementos in boxes in Daniel's mom, Anna's, storage. She was the only one that had space in the small apartments' storage rooms in Stockholm. She and I had always been very close, even after the divorce. I always saw her as my extra mom, and she's always cherished me like a daughter. Even now, we still chat sometimes.

Before I left, my family and friends hosted a going-away party for me at a Lebanese restaurant. It was a farewell filled with great Lebanese food, laughter, hugs, and many tears. Although I said again that I would be back in a year, everyone, including myself, knew I wouldn't. I did tell everyone that I would always come visit, and I wanted them to come visit me. I've kept my promise, as I've been going to Sweden at least once, if not twice a year, and they've visited me numerous times since I left. We also started a group chat on Facebook, one for my family "The Zeitos," our surname, and one for Adiba & Friends. I'm so grateful for this way of staying connected, as it would have been much harder to leave all my loved ones without getting continuous updates and pictures. By now, I had a nephew and my friends were starting to have children, so it felt even more important to get frequent updates.

On March 11, 2011, I landed in San Francisco, California, with my three suitcases and my dog Carmen, ready to begin my new life in America. My dream had finally come true.

# 19

## SILICON VALLEY: LIFE AND CAREER ON STEROIDS

Yes — I did it! All my years of working hard had finally paid off. I was now living in the U.S. and starting my career there. Before I arrived, I secured a small, end-unit apartment next to the AT&T Ballpark in San Francisco that had one bedroom, a kitchen, living room, and a washer and dryer. It was tiny but cost like $3,000 a month in rent, insanity! I had no furniture and only what I had brought with me in my three suitcases. I didn't know anyone there, only the few acquaintances I had made in the months prior and a guy friend, Paul, I knew earlier who lived close by.

Being that I am Swedish and this apartment was temporary, of course I headed to the Swedish IKEA to furnish my new place. I bought a couch, table, chairs, and a bed. Paul helped me assemble the (many!) pieces, and soon my apartment started to feel a little more like home. He also helped acclimate me to the social scene there. He not only introduced me to a lot of his friends, but he also invited me to join them when they all went out. This began a really fun time of going out to restaurants, nightclubs, and bars — just enjoying all this awesome city had to offer and getting to know new people, a new culture really. The San Francisco nightlife was a lot of fun; we partied mostly in the Marina though, as downtown was too touristy. I went on party bus trips to the wine country, and explored other beautiful places nearby with my new friends. Most of my new friends lived in the Marina, and since we mostly hung out there, I decided to rent a place there instead, just one block from the water with views of Golden Gate Bridge. The Marina reminded me of Kungsholmen, so I quickly felt at home there. I'm grateful to Paul for helping me make the transition to start a whole new life in the U.S. Because of him, it was smooth and filled with fun times. I'm so glad that he later met an amazing woman, Courtney, who became his wife and my best friend.

Most of my time I spent getting Innovative Sweden established in the U.S. I bought a used convertible Mini Cooper and named it "Mini Me" since it seemed to literally become an extension of me. I drove a *lot* to Silicon Valley and surrounding areas — I was always in that car going from meeting to meeting! I spent most of my time in the heart of Silicon Valley, in Palo Alto meeting people for coffee or lunch at University Café or Coupa Café or hanging out at Stanford University. I also had meetings in Mountain View, San Jose, Berkeley, and all of the other little towns in the area. Silicon Valley is spread out over a very large area, from San Francisco in the north to San Jose in the south. It was extremely inspiring to connect with everyone in the Silicon Valley ecosystem. I couldn't believe that this was now all part of my actual job. I had a constant smile on my face; I was so happy living the dream.

I made many connections and was able to get into most of the large tech companies where I got to see the future being made in front of my eyes. The campuses of some of the tech companies in Silicon Valley are like small villages. For instance, Google's Headquarters Googleplex in Mountainview has everything you need to stay at work 24/7 — fitness centers, pools, 25 cafés and restaurants, hair salon on wheels, different sport activities — and everything is free for employees. It is one of the coolest offices I've ever seen. There is nothing traditional about it, it's like an amusement park for geeks. The same goes for Facebook and Apple headquarters.

I was also super fascinated by Stanford and all the brainpower within its walls. Just a few blocks from there is where Steve Jobs invented the first personal computer in his garage. I spoke to many scientists and learned about technologies that had not yet hit the market but would definitely change the world as we knew it. I met with people at the research institute, SRI International, that has been the brains behind most of the tech innovations of the last 50 years. For instance, discovering that the Internet was invented there was pretty mind-blowing. A few years after I worked on different projects with these people, I saw the future generation of Artificial Intelligence up close with demonstrations of super smart robots doing things nobody could imagine. I drove the first Tesla Roadster that went from 0 to 100 miles per hour in mere seconds, taking my stomach with it! I saw tiny microchips at Singularity University that were being developed for the human body to release medicine, perform diagnostics, fight cancer, or provide a digital interface between brains and machines. A few years later, I became a mentor for startup entrepreneurs at Singularity

University's incubator. It was an amazing, magical experience to be a part of all they had going on. All these connections paid off, as I was now ready to launch Innovative Sweden. I hired an awesome marketing executive, a Swedish woman, Katarina, and signed a lease for a space in the newly opened co-working space, RocketSpace. It was a great space to be in, as I got to meet investors and startups and learn even more about how Silicon Valley works. Networking was key, so I attended at least one, sometimes two events a day where I connected with even more amazing people. In a very short time, I had created a healthy network of incredible people from every corner of Silicon Valley. It was hard to imagine just how much I saw and experienced, and the people I met in this very short time of my life. The plan was to launch Innovative Sweden in November, just eight months after I landed in San Francisco.

With many miles covered and mostly 10 to 14 hour work days, Innovative Sweden was ready to be launched on time. We were prepared with two weeks of seminars, programs, interviews, talks — a packed, informative schedule for participants. This visiting program initiated partnerships between Swedish and Silicon Valley companies and investors. Before Innovative Sweden, most of these awesome Swedish companies with impressive, innovative products were virtually unknown to Silicon Valley. We had now started the work of positioning Sweden as an attractive producer of innovation and technology in the world's hottest tech hub of Silicon Valley.

The November launch of Innovative Sweden was a great success. The roadshow continued to other countries and toured the World for four years, without me. I decided to stay in Silicon Valley, as I very much loved living and working here. I was approached by the president of Silicon Vikings, an organization that worked to connect all of the innovation and startup ecosystems in the Nordic countries with Silicon Valley and vice versa. He asked if I wanted to interview for the executive director role that was about to be vacant. I was also approached by U.S. Market Access Center, USMAC, that provides international tech companies with fast and successful access to the U.S. and global markets via Silicon Valley, to become their vice president of international relations. I was offered both jobs, but instead of choosing one of the positions, I agreed to take both of them, as the work hours were pretty flexible. Why not? I was young, single, super ambitious, and I loved this work. It made complete sense to me!

# 20

# THIRD AND BIGGEST LOVE YET:
## MARRIAGE TAKE 2

et me tell you how I met my amazing husband, Kris. Six months
after I arrived in San Francisco, I became curious about how
the dating culture works in the U.S. I hadn't had time to date
anyone, since I was so focused on getting Innovative Sweden up
and running. Working in a very male-dominated industry as a young
female, I, unfortunately, got hit on a lot. I often received nice
compliments, but there were times when the comments felt really
uncomfortable, and I had to say loud and clear, *I am not interested!* I
refused to go out with anyone that I was connected with through
work. I had always kept my professional and personal life separate.

Since I had success with Match.com before, I decided to give it
another go. I set up a U.S. account and profile and waited to see what
happened. I went out with a few guys, but nobody ever made it to
the second date. That is, not until I saw the profile of a guy named
Kris Barney. His photo was literally of his profile, so I couldn't see
his full face. It wasn't his looks that interested me in connecting, since

I couldn't really see what he looked like. The information he shared intrigued me. We seemed to have similar interests, but one thing stood out — he shared that he had recently been skydiving and that he wanted to learn to kitesurf. I had done a bit of kitesurfing with Magnus, and at the time, I was researching good skydiving options around the Bay Area. We started chatting about that via messenger on Match.com and eventually agreed to meet in person. He was seven years younger than me, but I didn't see that as a problem at all, as I've always felt younger than my age. Our plan was to meet and have one drink at the Cosmopolitan Bar near my office at RocketSpace. He was flying out the next day to go on a two-week vacation with his friends, so he said beforehand that he couldn't be out late. Well, that plan soon went out the window. There was an instant connection between us. We talked and talked, ended up having more drinks, then dinner and then more drinks. I was fascinated by this guy, he was smart, adventurous, handsome, and a bit shy in a nerdy kind of way. We agreed that we would see each other again after he returned from his trip. While Kris was away, he kept texting me photos of the beautiful scenery where he was, sunset photos and others. Yep, he was definitely into me.

We continued dating when he got back, and our relationship quickly grew serious. Without a doubt, I had fallen in love with this man! We loved hanging out together and exploring the Bay Area. We went on hikes in the beautiful Marin Headlands, and he showed me his favorite spots. He was a big hiker; I was not as much but still enjoyed it. He grew up in Dayton, Ohio, lived in Chicago after graduation, and had only lived in San Francisco for a year when we met, so there were a lot of new places we could explore together.

And then it came time to meet the parents. I was super nervous. I have no idea why, I just was. I had always had an easy time connecting with the "in-laws," as I'm a very social and outgoing person. With everyone I meet, I am always very personable, open about who I am, and then all huggy and voila, we are super close. But this was different. I had no idea how American parents would react to the girlfriend. The only knowledge I had of American parents was from American movies and television shows where the moms always seemed overprotective — no one was good enough for their baby. In the end, I was worried for no reason. Kris' parents, Kathy and Randy, and brothers, Kurt and Ken, were absolutely amazing from the start. They all laughed a lot and were just a very sweet and loving family. We connected right away. Pheew, check!

After a year of dating, we decided to move in together. We found a great one-bedroom place in Pacific Heights on Broadway Street. It was high up in a tall building that offered great views of the entire city and overlooked the water and Golden Gate Bridge from the rooftop. It was beautiful! My love for Kris grew even more, as he was a dream to live with, except for his lack of cleaning skills. Then it was time for me to bring Kris home to Sweden to meet my family and friends. He had no idea what he was in for, as my family is loud and super personal. We have zero shyness in our bodies, we just dive in and tell stories about the most embarrassing moments in each other's lives. We tease each other constantly, and we all revert into being five kids living in a house together and assume the roles we had growing up.

Kris right away felt welcomed into the family; after all, he now knew a lot about us in a very short time. He laughed out loud the whole night. Poor guy, he was exhausted after that first meeting. We can be pretty intense!

Our life together was beautiful and romantic, and our love for each other grew stronger and stronger. I loved how he always left little loving notes for me here and there. He would come up with the most creative surprise gifts that were all experiences and mini-adventures, as he knew I valued that way more than things or jewelry. I've never put any value in diamonds or fancy stuff or jewelry. Experiences to me have always had the highest value. I still liked getting roses now and then, and I would come home and find beautiful roses in a vase with cute, cheesy notes attached. He was and still is my biggest love! I had found the perfect guy, and I was so happy.

Kris proposed to me on August 25, 2013 and I of course said YES! Honestly, I had not thought I would ever remarry, but then I met Kris and fell madly in love. I definitely saw a future for us. I could see myself having a great life with Kris, growing old with him, having a family together. It also meant that I would most likely never move back to Sweden. Kris told me early on in our relationship that he could not see himself living in a country that had more winter than summer, that was one of the reasons he moved to California. So, back to the proposal — here is how it happened! I had just finished working on a huge project and was exhausted. I had woken up that morning with a fever and felt like crap. Kris said he had plans for us that day and that it would not be too tough on me. He said if I could humor him, he had a surprise for me. Like I said, he had always planned cute, little surprise happenings for me, so I didn't think more of it. We got in the car, and he gave me three books and then told me that I had to choose one. One book was about a dog being a man's best friend, one was sci-fi, and one was about a woman who liberated herself from the patriarchal society in the 1920s. I chose the last one. Then he told me to flip to a certain page, so I did. Next, he said I was to read sentence number something. I did, and it was the weirdest thing, as the woman in the book was reading a book about how it was OK for women to experience pleasure during sex and so on. I was like hmmm, where is he taking me... We drove over the Golden Gate Bridge and started driving up Mt. Tamalpais. Up and up we went. I was not feeling great, as I realized I had a really bad cold, probably the flu. We stopped at the highest spot you could take a car, above the fog. It was a really windy day. He took out a picnic blanket and laid out a picnic he had prepared. He could not get the blanket to lay flat, as the wind was blowing so hard. He tried and tried, but he couldn't keep the blanket down, so he asked me to sit on it. Then he went down on his knees and popped the question! I was like, *wow, it's happening right now, and my nose is super runny in this crazy wind.* I hardly heard what he said, the wind was so loud, but I just said YES! We started laughing and both said, "let's get out of here." Kris said, "I have a bottle of champagne, let's just toast, and then we can leave." He popped the cork, but because we had driven up the mountain to a higher altitude, the pressure was insanely high, and since the bottle was aimed at me, I got showered with champagne from head to toe! Hahaha! It was the most messed-up proposal, but I love it more, because it was a hilarious failure. Poor Kris, he felt so bad about all of it. He had planned it all so well, and even distracted me with all those books that had nothing to do with anything.

Around the same time as the proposal, I received a letter from the Cancer Center in Sweden notifying me that I had a clean bill of health. I was exhilarated! My last mammogram earlier that summer had been clear, and since it had now been five years since I finished treatment for my stage 1 breast cancer, I was now considered cured. However, they didn't do any body scans during this whole time, so they had no idea if the cancer was lurking somewhere else. We just assumed everything was clear, and cancer was gone forever.

Kris and I got married on December 7, 2013 at Paradise Ridge Winery in Sonoma Valley. We had a lovely, intimate ceremony with around 45 of our close family and friends there with us. We were so happy and in love. We decided that our wedding would just be all about dancing and having fun with our friends and family. Very little traditional wedding stuff was done; it was mostly a party with fancy clothes, beautiful scenery, and tasty food and wine. We danced for hours, and everyone was happy and laughing with us. It was perfect!

Right before we were married, I was approached by a very established Silicon Valley nonprofit organization called Silicon Valley Forum. They had been in existence for over 30 years and always had great leadership and a strong brand and reputation in the Valley. However, they had been part of what was referred to as "old" Silicon Valley. When I arrived in Silicon Valley, a new era of tech was booming. Social media and apps were taking off and San Francisco, SoMa, South of Market Street, had become a hub for these new tech companies. The new generation of Silicon Valley was taking over. By now, I had built a strong brand for myself. Silicon Valley Forum was looking for a new CEO to transform the organization, rejuvenate it, and make it more relevant in the "new" Silicon Valley. I had been recommended by several people in the industry who knew what I had accomplished in the short time I had been in Silicon Valley. That really meant a lot to me, considering that I had not been in Silicon Valley very long. The Board of Directors of Silicon Valley Forum was made up of incredible people in prominent positions at some of the giants in the tech industry, venture capital firms, law firms, and experienced entrepreneurs. I interviewed with several of them, and it was the most nervous I've ever been. But, I knew my strengths and was confident I could pull it off even though I was much younger and less experienced than previous CEOs in the organization's history. I presented them with ideas of how I would take the organization to the next level, build on the great legacy that Silicon Valley Forum had created over the past 30+ years, and how I would create exciting new directions for both members and partners going forward. With my international experience and connections, I shared how I could transform the organization from being a local player to having a global presence. It worked like a charm, because the next thing I knew, I was offered the job. All of this happened during our wedding week, which meant we were already all consumed with final wedding preparations, entertaining lots of family and friends who had flown in from Sweden, and, the most important event of all, our actual wedding!

While I was enjoying dinner with my Swedish besties at one of our pre-wedding dinners, I received a phone call from the Board

Chair of Silicon Valley Forum. We had not finalized the details of my employment package, so I stepped away, and I negotiated my salary and benefits while standing out on the street outside of the restaurant. Everything I had worked so hard for culminated in this moment. This position would be a great springboard for my career in Silicon Valley. I was going places. I had many goals and dreams for the next season of my career and my life. It really sucked that soon I would find out that I wouldn't be able to meet my goals and realize my career dreams, because a deadly disease would soon come and crush it all to pieces.

We had wanted to travel somewhere abroad for our honeymoon, but I was still in the process of getting my green card, so I couldn't leave the U.S. That travel would come later. We honeymooned in Maui, Hawaii, and enjoyed two fabulous weeks celebrating the beginning of married life. The trip was more than perfect! We were upgraded to the nicest suite with a Jacuzzi overlooking the ocean and had the best time relaxing on the beach, enjoying great food, seeing the sights, and just loving each other. Our honeymoon was one of the many fun adventures and travels we have done together. Traveling and collecting experiences has always been our thing and what we prefer to spend our money on. Besides Hawaii, a place we've been to three times, we have traveled to many places across Europe — Rome, Sicily, Paris, Athens, Santorini, and Copenhagen. We have been to Sweden many times and spent a lot of time in Stockholm with my family and friends. We have also been to the Ice hotel up North, above the Arctic Circle. In addition, we have been to Cabo and Cancun in Mexico, the Bahamas and Turks and Caicos in the Caribbean, and have explored a lot of places in the U.S., especially during a ten-day cross-country roadtrip. Our favorite spot in California is Laguna Beach in Orange County, where we have friends who live there. So many wonderful places and countless memories! Add all of these locations to the many places I had traveled to before I met Kris, and I have traveled to and seen much of our world. However, I still have destinations on my bucket list that I want to experience before I die. I still have plans to go on a safari in Africa, take an RV through New Zealand from north to south, and visit Japan, Fiji, Singapore, Vietnam, and Machu Picchu in Peru. In fact, Kris was going to take a six-month sabbatical that would have allowed us to do a mini tour around the world from May through October 2020, but then Covid put a stop to our plans.

Back to 2013 — I started my new job with Silicon Valley Forum soon after we returned from our honeymoon. Kris is a finance guy and was in the investment banking industry at the time, so between our two demanding careers, we both worked so hard. We made spending time together a priority and carved out time for our travels, dinner dates, and special outings and experiences together. We share so many similar interests — we are both Sci-Fi fans, love Marvel and all the superheroes, and are big movie fans, so we were always the first ones at the opening night of every new Marvel or Sci-Fi release. Golf was also something we enjoyed together, although I really sucked at the game. He has always been way better than me at it. Yes! I admit it baby! The only great achievement I've had in golf is a hole-in-one I made while playing a company golf tournament in Sweden in, I believe, 2004. It was a funny story, as I had started playing golf just to be able to host this tournament called Kistaslaget. It was organized annually for all the executives at the companies in Kista Science City.

I had never thought about playing golf, as I was more of a fast sports kind of person, and golf seemed lame to me. Since my employer had been hosting this tournament every year, I was asked to organize it as part of my role with Kista Science City. In Sweden, you can't play golf if you don't have a so-called green card. To get a green card, you had to take classes to learn how to play the game of golf as well the rules of the game and etiquette on the course. Then you had to pass both a written test and a test demonstrating your golf skills in order to receive the card. I did not want to appear to be completely clueless about the sport, especially since I was organizing a golf tournament, so I did what I needed to do to get the green card. I was a complete rookie and was pretty lousy at playing, so for me to make a hole-in-one had nothing to do with talent, it was just pure luck. Over a hundred people, mostly men since the tech industry was male dominant, celebrated my HiO at the after-party. I was the talk of the town for a long time after as the HiO girl. Most people had no idea how lousy I actually was at the game, haha. I think there is still a HiO placard at Lindö GK with my name on it.

# UNFUCKWITHABLE

Now that's a word that totally encapsulates how I always try to live my life and one that has absolutely helped in my career, my fight for independence, and throughout my whole cancer journey.

If you look it up in a slang dictionary, you'll find the following: "Unfuckwithable is when you are truly at peace with yourself, and nothing anyone says or does bothers you, no negativity or drama can touch you."

It took a while and several disappointments to get to the point in my life when I said, *nope, not gonna let that bother me.* Not gonna let that boss or that colleague get to me — working as a young, female executive in the tech industry forced me to really embrace that mentality. I often found myself having to speak up and not care about how I would be perceived by my colleagues. If I didn't, I would not have gone far in my career. I was often seen as someone who was too forward, too much, took up too much space. It wasn't until I started working in Silicon Valley that I felt that I belonged, as most everyone there had that attitude. I realized that I was pretty normal for someone who was ambitious and wanted to go places. Don't be afraid to take up as much space as you like to get where you want in life. Speak up and make yourself heard, whether it's in your professional life, as a patient having to deal with many doctors' opinions on your care, or in your relationship where you feel you are not being heard and appreciated. It doesn't mean you don't care about people and their feelings. It doesn't mean you step on people to get there. In fact, you get way more done if, at the same time, you are kind, compassionate, and empathetic to other people's needs. You just don't want to lose yourself in the process.

# 21

# SILICON VALLEY:
## CAREER ON STEROIDS PART 2

So, fast forward to 2015. Kris and I were continuing to stay on the go, busy with our careers and having fun. Our life was pretty exciting and full! The last two years working as the CEO at Silicon Valley Forum had been a dream — I was in my element! This was definitely a job made for me, both when it came to my capabilities and my personality. I loved the challenge of completely restructuring the organization, rebranding it and transforming parts of it to adapt to a whole new market and generation. It was not an easy task, and I certainly made some enemies along the way, because not everyone agreed to the numerous changes that had to be made. However, I knew I was doing what was necessary to take us to the next level. Together with my talented and awesome team and my badass board, we created magic! We repositioned ourselves as one of the leading organizations that offered high-quality conferences on trending and future technologies. We provided our partners with many added benefits through our valuable connections with Silicon

Valley's different stakeholders. We supported startups from all over the world and enabled them to connect with venture capitalists, angel investors, and large corporations, and we became a go-to partner for innovation agencies from all over the world that wanted to connect with and learn from Silicon Valley.

My weekdays were insane, filled with meetings and "making things happen" activities. I had to leave our home in San Francisco no later than 6:30 a.m., as our office was in San Jose, about 50 miles (80km) away, and I absolutely hated sitting in traffic. The rush hour traffic in the Bay Area was a significant challenge when I first moved to San Francisco in 2011, but over the four years I had been there, it had gotten so much worse. There had been serious growth in the area since San Francisco had become part of the tech boom and was now a very popular hotspot, which brought in more people and many more cars.

Many of the new hot companies were headquartered in San Francisco, companies like Twitter, Uber, Airbnb, Zynga, Yelp — the list goes on. Because of this, startup accelerators and coworking spaces started popping up everywhere in the city as aspiring entrepreneurs from all over the world flocked to San Francisco to start the next Google or Facebook. The large and more established tech companies, headquartered farther south in Silicon Valley, started opening satellite offices in San Francisco as well. The Silicon Valley venture capital followed. In other words, traffic in the whole Bay Area was out of control, and because of the influx of people in the area, the housing market absolutely exploded. The growth in San Francisco caused an increased growth in the rest of Silicon Valley, as well as in the East

Bay area, where you have Oakland and Berkley. Basically wherever you wanted to go, you got stuck in traffic. Therefore, I preferred to leave early and come home late to avoid the worst of it, which gave me plenty of time to work. I honestly loved it so much that I didn't really mind. My enormous passion and drive for my job was still part of who I was, and that showed in my work. I got shit done, and I was high on endorphins from finishing one project after the other.

A big part of my job was getting up on stage and speaking in front of a lot of people, and I absolutely loved it. I felt at home on stage.

From the time I started working in the tech industry almost two decades earlier, one of my most favorite things to do was to coach startup entrepreneurs from all over the world and help them create the perfect pitch to present to investors. Unfortunately, I didn't get to do that as much in my role at Silicon Valley Forum, as it was not exactly a CEO task, but I still tried to fit it in here and there since I enjoyed it so much. Meeting entrepreneurs and government agency representatives for innovation from all over the world was always an eye-opening experience. From Brazil to New Zealand, Africa to Kazakhstan — incredible entrepreneurs and innovative startups could be found in every corner of the world. Silicon Valley was far from the only place that had the entrepreneurial spirit. I, of course, already knew that the Nordics and my Sweden are big tech and innovation hubs, but it was humbling to meet so many amazing people from other places. I just felt so inspired and learned so much from all the incredibly brilliant people I met on a daily basis in my job. I was lucky that my job allowed me to meet and chat with many of the mind-blowing visionaries in Silicon Valley. For over twenty years, we recognized a visionary at our annual Visionary Awards — industry leaders who have pioneered innovation and fostered the spirit of entrepreneurship, and whose unique vision continues to shape Silicon Valley. People like Esther Dyson, Elon Musk, Bill Gates, Ann Winblad, Steve Wozniak, Carly Fiorina, Anne Wojcicki, Vint Cerf, Heidi Rozen, Reid Hoffman, Reed Hastings, Marc Benioff, Salman Khan, Padma Warrior, Peter Diamandis, Ray Kurzweil, Jessica Jackley, Tony Fadell, Megan Smith, and about 90 other incredible role models are among this group of distinguished honorees.

There are also so many inspiring people who helped me along the way that I would like to thank, and those who were like mentors to me during my fast-paced and exciting years in Silicon Valley. You all know who you are! I thank you from the bottom of my heart for the experience of a lifetime!

Naturally, not everything was good. There were some things I hated about Silicon Valley. The fact that it still has, in this day and age, a "tech bro culture" always got to me. I didn't experience this part myself, as I had always held leading positions in the industry and had worked and negotiated with my board that was diverse and gender equal. In fact, a software platform study (Carta) that analyzed more than 6,000 companies, 180,000 employees, and 15,000 founders found that women in Silicon Valley earn less than their male counterparts and are awarded far less equity. I'm a feminist and have always fought hard for equal pay, and never shied away from negotiating my worth. To all women, I say go out there and demand equal pay! Stand up for yourself and what you believe you should earn and negotiate until you get it. Practice on a friend or family member, just make sure you don't just give in and take what's offered. It is your right, take it!

Another tough aspect of Silicon Valley, or more like globally, that has always bugged me is the fact that there are still very few female founders who receive funding. Only 2.8% of the U.S. Venture Capital invested in 2019 went to female founders, a percentage that is not due to a lack of female founders. I personally know many brilliant female founders who have struggled to raise capital, and told me horror stories of how discriminating the whole process has been. If everyone looked at the data, they would realize what a big mistake it is to not invest in a female founder's company. According to Boston Consulting Group, businesses founded by women deliver more than twice as much per dollar invested than those founded by men. Silicon Valley still has a long way to go before it removes the annoying patriarchal and tech bro culture and becomes a more equal community.

Within the Silicon Valley culture, sexual harassment continues to be a significant problem. Any type of sexual harassment or overall sexist behavior needs to be completely eradicated. It is never acceptable on any level. Period. I recall a few times when some older men during events or meetings would get a bit handsy or over-compliment my looks. I told them off without even allowing them a second to say another word. Zero tolerance!

# 22

# LET'S HAVE A BABY!
## COME ON, GIVE ME A FUCKING BREAK!!!

Kris and I loved our fast-paced careers and were enjoying a fun, active life in San Francisco, but we knew we wanted more. We both wanted to start a family. For the last two years, we had not been doing anything that would prevent us from getting pregnant. I never lost hope that one day I would become a mother. When I was single, I remember saying that even if I did not meet someone to have a baby with before I turned 40, I would adopt as a single mom

After a while, a familiar wave of grief returned when I started questioning why, after all this time, I wasn't getting pregnant. Yet again, a huge disappointment filled me, a feeling that, by now, I was used to when I thought of making babies. Kris knew about my previous years of trying and failing over and over again to have a baby, so we decided to go to a fertility clinic and signed up to begin IVF treatments. This would be the third time making embryos in a lab with someone. I knew that world well, and it sucked that I had to go through it again. We both really wanted a baby. Kris wasn't worried at all, but my history made me worry. We both had tests and were thoroughly screened — my eggs were still good, and his sperm was strong, so there shouldn't be a problem. The only thing they noticed was that my cervix was a little askew, which really wasn't an issue. For so many years, I had wanted a child, and for so many years, I desperately tried to have one. Now, at 37 years of age, I was starting the process all over again, but now I was much older and less fertile.

Before I started taking the hormone injections, the clinic wanted to make sure everything was OK on the breast cancer front, so they made me have a mammogram. I told them I had received a letter from the clinic in Sweden two years earlier letting me know that I had a clean bill of health, but they still wanted to make sure before starting me on hormonal stimulation treatments. I am so thankful they did, otherwise I might not be here today. The mammogram showed something small in my right, previously healthy, breast. Really? Give me a fucking break! The other breast too! I had a biopsy, and they determined it was super early, stage 0. They said all I needed to do this time was a mastectomy, removing the whole breast. No need for any other treatments, as it was such an early stage. I knew it was going to suck to not have functioning breasts, no sensation at all, two dead breasts. Even so, I said yes. *Let's just get rid of this cancer once and for all. Enough! I didn't want to deal with this ever again.*

·

# 23

# BREAST CANCER STRIKE 3:
## SENTENCED TO DEATH AT 37

Knowing that I would lose my second breast made me sad. Dealing with all of the emotions and everything surrounding the surgery and recovery was tough, but I was more focused on having a baby. Since having a mastectomy was the only thing standing in the way of me starting the process again to have a baby, I was ready to have the surgery. The sooner, the better. I was ready to be a mom.

Before my surgery, Kris and I met with one of the best plastic surgeons in the country, who was very good looking I might add, at the University of California San Francisco Health (UCSF). Anyone who has gone through even part of what I have with breast cancer knows that your breasts somehow become no longer your own. You seem to lose all modesty when it comes to doctors touching, prodding, or handling them. I remember the plastic surgeon drawing on my breast during our appointment and seeing Kris' face — awkward! *Someone was drawing on my wife's breast!*

The goal was to try to fix my breasts so they would be symmetrical. Unfortunately, my hard and immobile left breast was so badly damaged from the radiation I had in 2005 that the skin wouldn't stretch. So the effort to restore my left breast was not successful. However, reconstruction of my right breast was a great success; it was soft and had movement like a natural breast. Technology has advanced a lot since then, so today women have an even better chance at having good reconstruction results. Unfortunately, they still haven't figured out how to prevent the nerves in the breast from being damaged so sensation can be retained. At least I haven't heard of a procedure with results like that. I consider myself lucky that my nipples were spared with both mastectomies.

As I had remembered from before and expected, the recovery after a mastectomy and subsequent reconstruction was long and painful. My mom and Kris' parents stayed with us after my surgery, which was really nice. One day, a few days into my recovery, I had severe shortness of breath. I was so scared. Kris rushed me to the emergency room, where they did a CT scan. The doctors saw fluid around my lung and easily drained it so I could breathe again. Unfortunately, they saw something else. The more terrifying news was that the scan showed several spots on my spine and pelvis. I had never had a full body scan to determine if cancer was anywhere else in my body, as usually, just mammograms are done as follow-up when you have had breast cancer. I had been told I was cured. Nobody told me there was any risk that cancer could be growing somewhere else in my body, especially since my breast cancer had been early stage with tiny tumors both times. Since my lymph nodes had been all clear, I convinced myself they were most likely not cancerous tumors.

The fact is, about 30% of early stage breast cancer survivors, even after successful and completed treatments, will develop metastatic breast cancer at some point in their lives. It can happen right away or even as long as twenty years after. I had no idea, as no one had ever told me this, and nowhere in all the material I read about breast cancer did I see that specific fact. I didn't think anymore of it and went home thinking everything was good.

The next day, I received the most surreal phone call of my life. The news from the radiologist was unbelievable: they were pretty certain I had metastasis in my bones. But how? When? Why? They told me that the cancer cells had most likely traveled through my blood back in 2008, maybe earlier. They had been dormant, waiting, so it was difficult to know when they started metastasizing. Really!? I had stage 4, metastatic breast cancer. Did I just get sentenced to death? There is no cure! I'm only 37. This was the absolute worst news I could have ever received. No more future. I was never going to be a mom! The only question was — when would it kill me? Kris and I could not believe it. We both collapsed on the floor, holding each other. We were in shock and did not want to accept the news. *This can't be happening.* I recall hearing my mom and Kris' mom crying in the background. That's all I remember from those days. The days when I realized that I might not live to see my 40th birthday, knowing I will die young!

# 24

# METASTATIC BREAST CANCER AND ME:
## HOW DO YOU EVEN LIVE WITH THIS?

After receiving the devastating diagnosis that I had metastatic breast cancer, I met with a doctor who would become my hero oncologist at UCSF. She said, "I'm not going to sugarcoat it. Yes, you do have a deadly, incurable disease, and you will not get out alive. But, let's see just how long we can keep you here." Kris and I sat there, still in shock, with tears glistening in our eyes. We wanted to know how long I had to live. She let us know that it was hard to give an exact life prognosis, but that the statistics say two to three years, on average. She went on to say that life expectancy is very individual, and there were several treatment options and even some clinical trials I may be eligible to be a part of. Everything depended on how I responded to the treatments. I also learned that there would never be an end to treatment. I would be in treatment until I've exhausted them all, and there is nothing left for me to try. First, we needed to determine what subtype my cancer was. It could still be hormone sensitive, ER+/PR+, HER-, like it was when I was early stage, but it could have mutated and become a different subtype. We needed to do a biopsy of the bone. It was not an easy feat, since they had to drill into my spine and scrape off as much of the tumor tissue as possible. Yes, it is as horrible as it sounds, a really unpleasant experience. My oncologist was surprised that I didn't feel more pain in my back, for years, considering one of the tumors was about 5cm in my T4, pressing against my spinal cord. It must have been there for a while. Sure, I had felt some aches in my back but attributed it to working so hard, sitting in front of my computer, and the long drives back and forth to the office. Not in a million years did I think that the pain I was feeling was because cancer was eating away at my bones. We had to take care of that immediately, since that T4 tumor was millimeters away from paralyzing me.

I was scheduled to do an SBRT radiosurgery, which basically meant they would deliver one super high dose of radiation instead of giving me radiation treatments every day over a two- to four-week period. This procedure would concentrate the combined amount of radiation I would have received over a several-week period and give it to me in one session, so they could blast the tumor and eliminate it right then. This radiosurgery was part of a clinical study, so I had to sign like a hundred different documents. Before doing the procedure, I was immediately put on an anti-hormonal treatment called Tamoxifen, a medicine I had taken and hated in the past. They also started me on bone strengthening injections and a bunch of other pills.

It took forever until I finally got scheduled to do the radiosurgery. It ended up frying my nerves in the area and caused me to completely lose the use of the left side of my body, from my feet up to my T4 vertebrae. With this loss and weakness so severe on my right side, I was unable to walk and ended up having to use a wheelchair to get around. I had to go to physical therapy several times a week and do lots of exercises until I learned how to walk again. I went from using a wheelchair to walking with the support of a cane to finally walking with a limp. A limp I still have to this day. It wasn't easy to go from being fully mobile to having a disability, but I have always been strong and determined, and I don't easily give up. I started using all kinds of methods to strengthen my body so I could walk again. I bought a leg exerciser that I would sit in a chair and pedal on every day. Each day, I added more and more time. I started doing yoga frequently. The hard work paid off, even if I still walk with a limp. I may not be able to run or jump or do any movements that require that kind of balance, as I basically don't have any, but I am now able to walk pretty fast.

The pain from the nerve damage was the worst and never went away. It actually just got worse and worse, and the sensation on my left side never returned. I was told the nerve damage was permanent. I've been on every pain medicine you can imagine. Today, I take eleven pills for pain management on a daily basis, and I still have more pain than most people would normally be able to tolerate. Pain has become part of my life. I honestly don't remember what it feels like to not have pain, which is probably for the best.

We decided to move to a more calm and serene environment, and had always been in love with Marin County. It is a beautiful area with gorgeous hills, water views, and boat marinas that you can see just beyond the Golden Gate Bridge. Before I got sick, we had been planning to buy a house in Sausalito, Tiburon, or Mill Valley, but that all changed as we didn't know how long I had left to live or what kind of medical bills we would have in the future. Fortunately, we both had the best medical insurance through work, so we knew most of my medical expenses would be covered. We found a cute, small, three-bedroom house for rent that faced the water in Tiburon on Paradise Drive, a place we had gone biking a lot. We moved in pretty quickly, as I just needed to get away from all the stress in the city. The area was so beautiful and green, and the water views were amazing. The hummingbirds loved the trees we had next to our big patio, and I loved watching them. I even dressed in a full red outfit, from head to toe, so I could get really up close and take pictures of them. We also enjoyed frequent visits from families of deer that looked like the children's book character, Bambi. I really needed to live in this piece of paradise. We also added to our family when we rescued a miniature pinscher/chihuahua mix puppy we named Sky. From the moment she came into our lives, she literally showered us with love via an abundance of wet kisses. Her sister Carmen was not very happy about this crazy, overly energetic little thing coming in and basically taking over the house. The two of them added a lot of great energy to our house, which was welcomed.

My first line of treatment, Tamoxifen, was intended to put me into menopause, since my cancer cells feed on estrogen and grow. Unfortunately, after only seven months, the treatment failed. A scan showed that I had a few spots in one of my lungs. There was a new

FDA-approved treatment that had promising results in the market, a CDK inhibitor, that was taken as a pill everyday. I found out that I was eligible to take it, and it could potentially add another 22 months to my life. The pill was called Ibrance, which I took in combination with an Aromatase Inhibitor called Letrozole that would make sure that no estrogen was produced in my body. Before I could start this new treatment, I had to be post-menopausal, and the only way to make that happen was to remove my ovaries. Well, it's not like I had a choice in the matter at this point. More about this later.

I didn't want to give up on my career, so I tried to combine treatments and my busy hospital schedule with my even more hectic work schedule for a full year. I even kept accepting speaking engagements and went on a work trip to New Zealand with one of my closest Venture Capital friends. We toured all of New Zealand's startup and innovation scene, meeting with their investors and their government agency for innovation. We listened to numerous startups pitch at several incubators in the country and gave them feedback. I remember crashing hard at the hotel each night, as I was exhausted beyond measure. Before cancer treatments came into my life, I had so much energy, and busy days like that wouldn't affect me at all. Now I struggled, and even though everyone I worked with knew about my cancer, they didn't know how hard it was for me to keep up. They just saw the person I've always been, what I wanted them to see. It had taken me almost two years to transform the organization, rebrand us, and make us a relevant player on the international scene. I didn't want to give that up. I believed I could do it all, or at least I tried to convince myself I could. I did not want cancer to take that away from me.

Over time, it just became too hard. I started working mostly from home and scheduled fewer meetings. It was taking more and more of a toll on me. I did not want to resign, so I decided instead that I would take short-term disability, because I still held out hope that I would come back. Short-term eventually turned into long-term disability. Luckily, throughout my career, I had always trained the person who worked closest to me to do my job in case of an emergency. I had trained my COO, Denyse, at Silicon Valley Forum long before I got sick, as I've always believed that an organization should not risk falling without its leader. You never know when something like that might happen. I also wanted to feel like I could disappear and go on vacation without feeling the stress that the organization could not function without me. So she was well-prepared to step in when I went on sick leave, and to take over my job later when I resigned. I had an amazing dream team who managed the organization in an exemplary fashion in my absence.

After a while, I realized that as much as I wanted to continue working, I just couldn't do it any longer. This was one of the most difficult decisions I have ever had to make. I went through a very tough identity crisis. My career was officially over in February of 2016, the same time my dream of ever becoming a mother was shattered. It was all too much. I broke down and moved into a very dark, depressed stage in my life. My career had been so important to me for so long, and I had a lot more I wanted to accomplish. I loved being busy and working in the thick of everything in Silicon Valley. I had worked so hard to build a successful career. My job was so much of who I was. I loved everything about it. *Who was I without my job? What am I? Am I just the constant cancer patient?* My time previously spent in exciting meetings with people who had great visions and ideas was now spent sitting in waiting rooms, waiting to get my blood drawn, my blood pressure checked, and meeting with the numerous doctors, each specialists for different parts of my body. I was constantly moving further away from the world I had known and loved. That world and the one I now lived in seemed light years apart. I had a hard time understanding what my purpose was and who I was in this world now. I would also never fulfill my ultimate dream of creating an Impact Investing Fund that only invested in startups that had world-changing products and solutions. Companies that I believed could make a great impact on our planet, and at the same time generate good profits. I felt so lost. I also had to face the fact that I will die much sooner than I ever imagined. Added to my identity crisis now was an intense bout of death anxiety. This was a tough and dark time in my life, and I had to do something to get out of it.

I realized that I had to find a new purpose, find a way to activate myself, and use whatever energy I had to do something meaningful. Something that would reignite my passion and fire. I had never been good at doing nothing. I decided to sit on a few boards. Earlier, I had been a board member at the Swedish American Chamber of Commerce, and had now become their chair. Most of all though, I wanted to make an impact in the Metastatic Breast Cancer (MBC) community. I decided to reach out to the Executive Director of Susan G. Komen in San Francisco and asked if I could be of any help, but made it clear that I only wanted to focus my efforts on MBC. The pink ribbon campaigns about early detection and general information about breast cancer in its early stages had enough attention out there. Those of us living with the deadly and incurable MBC were pretty much invisible within this organization or any other breast cancer awareness efforts. It was as if no one wanted to acknowledge and talk about the people that breast cancer actually killed. MBC is so far from the pink tata campaigns where it's all about making witty taglines and warrior poses. We are NOT breast cancer survivors, we are dying sooner or later, yet every time the media mentioned one of us, they would use the word "survivor." They even go as far as to say, "We wish you a healthy recovery," as if we're ever going to recover. Only 22% of us live longer than five years, and as few as 11% longer than ten years. That means that if I'm not among the 11%, I will die before my son turns seven. Anyway, I was asked to join their board and started coming up with ideas for MBC awareness campaigns. We organized the first MBC Conference in the Bay Area, and I joined the California advocacy group at Komen. I went to Washington, DC and walked the corridors of the Congressional and Senate office buildings to talk to the California representatives. I was interviewed for several different media outlets and started telling my story. All of my efforts made me feel so much better. I finally found that I had a place in this world again.

# HOPE IS MORE POWERFUL THAN WE GIVE IT CREDIT FOR

Throughout the years of challenges, HOPE has been my best friend. I don't know exactly at what point I started to put my trust and belief in hope, but I know that I would not have made it this far without it. We need hope to be able to cope with whatever life throws at us. Hope that everything will work out. But hope can't do the work for you, you need to believe in your own ability to make it happen, and hope will be there to comfort you in the meantime.

Throughout my life, there have been two main areas where hope has played a big role. First in my struggle with breast cancer, twice as a stage 1 survivor, and since 2015 with the deadly stage 4 diagnosis. I hope to continue living. I hope that each line of treatment works longer. I hope that my quarterly scans show stable results. Even if the treatments and the numerous surgeries are super tough, I'm hoping that they will grant me a longer life, to be there for my loved ones. Hope keeps me going.

The second struggle that was part of my life for fifteen years was my longing for a baby, to have a family of my own. With all the challenges and tough struggles I've had in my life, nothing hurt me as much as not being able to have a child. It was the absolute biggest source of grief in my life. After all the months of trying, year after year, even with the help of the latest IVF, it just didn't happen. However, I never gave up hope that one of these days I would be a mommy. And, today I am. Not giving up hope for so long did finally pay off. The day I looked into my baby boy's eyes for the first time and held him in my arms, was, by far, the most amazing and fulfilling experience in my life. He is my everything, my biggest love, my greatest accomplishment, my heart and my soul, and I have hope to thank for that. I could have given up hope, but I didn't, and I was rewarded for it.

# 25

## THREE FROZEN EMBRYOS:
## THERE IS STILL HOPE IN A FREEZER

The surgery to have my ovaries removed was scheduled. Before that, they suggested that I check with my fertility doctor to see if any of my eggs could be saved. This brought up both some really tough feelings and some hope. After this surgery, I would never be able to carry a child. I mean, I knew this logically, but the surgery made it more final and hurt my heart on a deeper level. BUT, IF there was ever any chance of having a baby in the future, we absolutely wanted to find out!

We met with a fertility oncologist, a badass in the field named Dr. Rosen. Without stimulating me with too many hormones, just the absolute minimum, since I couldn't feed my cancer cells with estrogen, he was able to harvest three eggs from my ovaries that were all a good grade, which gave me hope. He said the chance of us getting pregnant was however extremely low, only 7% per embryo. We fertilized them with Kris' sperm and froze them at the clinic, giving us a tiny glimmer of hope for the future. Before this happened, we did not think there was a chance we would have a baby. Of course, this news added tons of happiness hormones to my life, because there was still hope. *Even if the chances were low, I would take it!*

However, Kris and I still had to have the hard talk and figure out what we were going to do. Was it fair to bring a baby into this world? We had so much to think about before we were even close to making such a huge decision. We decided to have my ovaries removed and then start my second line of treatment before coming to a final answer. We really hoped that this treatment would do better than the previous one so I would be able to live longer and maybe, just maybe, become a mother.

# 26

## MEMORY BANK OVERLOAD: TRAVELS AND FUN WITH LOVED ONES

esides finding a new purpose in my life, I knew I needed to brighten my days with having fun experiences, traveling to great destinations, and creating even more amazing memories with my loved ones. Being depressed was not something I would allow to continue in my life. Every other time I had faced difficult challenges, I had refused to let myself stay in a dark place. Yes, my dreams were shattered, but I was determined to feel happiness again. I believe we have power over how we feel, we can manipulate our brain and choose how to think about what we're going through. Of course, if the depression is clinical and professional help is needed, that is different. I think most people who are unhappy walk around thinking negative thoughts, choose to see darkness instead of light, and choose to dwell in their misery instead of actively changing their situation.

I decided to start thinking about all the amazing experiences I had had in my lifetime. It was amazing how many wonderful and incredible things had happened in my relatively short life; I wasn't even 40. I realized that I had squeezed more into my life than most people did in an entire lifetime. I decided right then and there that I was not dead yet, so I would not act like I was. I had to keep living while I could. I decided I was actually going to live the HELL out of life! I was going to do things I had never had time to do before because I had always been working. Now I was on disability, and I had no responsibilities. I had never had time for hobbies or other travels with family and friends, but I did now. Naturally when Kris and I had our short vacations, we traveled somewhere just the two of us. Now I wanted to travel and create fun memories with all of my loved ones. I decided I was going to act as if I was in retirement, a retirement full of activity and joy! I didn't want anyone to remember me as being sad and the one who gave up on life. No, I changed my outlook and took control of my life again. Time was precious. Who knows how much longer I have left on this Earth.

The chat group I had on Facebook with my eleven closest Swedish friends called Adiba & Friends really helped me through this tough time. My amazing friends really know me, and they knew what I needed to feel better. I had kept them updated on all that was going on in my life. I don't remember who suggested it, but we decided to start a new tradition and see different parts of the world together on annual girls' trips. Exactly what I needed! The first trip took place in May of 2016. We went to Anna Maria Island in Florida, rented a big house steps from the beach, and had the most amazing time! I am so grateful that I have such amazing and caring friends in my life. No matter how far we are from each other, we are always there for one another. Even before I got sick, they would visit me either one-on-one or in a larger group on a regular basis. We would get into my Mini Me or rent a bigger van and go on roadtrips along Highway 1, do SoCal, Vegas, or just explore the Bay Area together. Every time I visit Sweden, the whole gang meets up several times, and we really max out our time together. We had already experienced so many beautiful and fun memories together, and I was ready to add even more. I'm living on borrowed time, so I know that all of the memories of us spending time together will be important to all my loved ones when I pass away. They will be able to look back on our time together and recall all of the recent, fun travels we have enjoyed together.

I decided to do the same thing with my family. Cozette, my brother's fiancé (at the time) and I went to Isla Holbox outside the Yucatan in Mexico. Even more amazing memories were added to my memory bank during that trip.

One of the more surprising trips I decided I wanted to take that same year was when I went to Lebanon with my brother, my parents, and my uncle and his wife. It was the first time I had been back to my birth country since we escaped in 1984. It was the first time for my brother too, as we were the only ones among us kids that were old enough to remember anything about Lebanon. We went back to see where we lived in Beirut, and actually got to go inside the exact apartment. I didn't know this, but friends of my parents were living in the same apartment we had lived in, so they let us inside. It was surreal to see it. It looked much smaller than I had remembered it being. I recall that my grandma and grandpa on my dad's side were living with us in that apartment. I went out to the balcony and memories just flooded me. I immediately recalled the times we would tie a rope around a bucket and lower it down to ground level, where my grandpa would put the groceries he had purchased from the market into the bucket so he didn't have to carry them up all the way up the stairs. The rooms and the kitchen also brought back memories. It was as if I had gone back in time. I had flashbacks of standing on a stool and doing dishes in the kitchen; I must not have been tall enough to reach the sink. I asked to also see the underground shelter that basically was our second home, where we hid during the bombings. Unfortunately, I only got to see the steel door, since it was locked, and we couldn't explore the inside. Maybe it was for the best, as it would have probably brought up too many tough memories that I've suppressed as a child. My parents took me to each part of Beirut that had meaning to our lives. We could still see holes from where the missiles had hit in many of the buildings that must not have been completely destroyed and therefore not rebuilt. We also went to the beach, where I have many fond memories, and also up the beautiful mountains and past all the vineyards. We ate so much super yummy Lebanese food and drank Lebanese wine. You could hear music and celebration everywhere. It was hard to see everything and process the gravity of it all, but it was part of my history. Beirut is a beautiful city, and it actually reminded me a lot of the San Francisco Bay Area with the surrounding water, all the hills, the wine country, and winding roads up the mountain. I was really happy that I took this trip and finally got to see Beirut from a peaceful perspective. I'm surprised that I didn't feel any kinship with the country, or a feeling of coming home at all. It was a completely strange country to me. For me, Sweden is and will always be my home country.

In December 2016, my Swedish best friends sent me a big care package. Inside were 24 different gifts, all numbered, one to be opened each day leading up to Christmas. One of the gifts was a notebook, and on the inside it said, "'When life hands you cactuses, make margaritas.' You keep talking about writing a book and this is the title you always said your book would have. Now, write your book." This was just the push I needed. I had talked about writing a book for a long time, but never did. I posted it on Facebook, to see if there was any interest at all, and my friends and colleagues all responded with, "DO IT!" Some said create a page so they could pre-order copies. I listened to them and started a campaign on Indiegogo to help raise money for the book and sell copies in advance. I ended up selling over $13,000 worth of books! My friends have always believed in me and knew I could do it. They were right, but I didn't realize how hard it would be to write a book about my life. I started, and it went really well for a while. And then I just couldn't do it anymore. I just couldn't write one more word. Maybe subconsciously I knew that my story was missing something big, and the most magical milestone in my life had not yet happened.

# 27

# SURROGACY:
## THE PURSUIT OF THE PERFECT WOMB TO CARRY OUR CHILD

In August 2016 something absolutely amazing happened: my quarterly scan showed no sign of any tumors in my whole body. I was officially tumor free, or, what it is normally called, NEAD, No Evidence of Active Disease. In other words, I was responding really well to the Ibrance+Letrozole treatment that I had been on since the beginning of the year. Woohoo! This gave me hope. It gave us hope. Kris and I were really happy that I was finally getting some good news. I was not going to die yet! There were no guarantees, and my oncologist was clear about that, but she also said that it would be a great time to pursue any life plans we had, as it looked like I was going to be here for a while. Well, there was only one life plan that we had been thinking about a lot since we harvested my eggs and froze those three embryos. We knew that this was it.

This could be the sign we needed. Could we now really pursue our ultimate dream of having a child? Was it the right thing for us to do?

I felt like I had achieved a lot in my life. I've had a very full life. I had built an amazing career, seen the world, had great loves, but there had always been this big hole in my heart. A missing piece, since I was 25 years old — I wanted a child, I wanted to become a mother. After everything I had been through, that had always been the source of my biggest grief. Now I was almost 40. Would it be fair to have a child knowing that I would not be around as long as I would want, as long as that child would need? The odds are against me: only 22% of people with MBC live longer than five years; only 11% longer than ten years. I had the absolute hardest decision of my life to make. I felt so much guilt for wanting to bring a child into all this. So many questions were going through my head. What if I died before my child can even remember me? Is that maybe better than remembering me? How would my death affect my child? What would Kris' life look like as a widowed dad? I saw a therapist to help me work through all these feelings. If I didn't do it, would I feel regret? There are a few people who have lived almost twenty years with this disease, so what if I lived for a very long time? If I were one of these people, would I live all this time regretting not having a child and grieving for the chance lost? If I did do it, would I feel guilty about it all the time? Could I live with that? I realized that a child would always be missed in my life, and a child would be so very much loved by Kris and I, more than that child could ever imagine. Kris had been struggling with the same questions and thoughts as I had, and luckily, besides me, had great friends he could talk to about it. He was also scared that

I would pass before our child was even born, since this process would take some time. The thought of becoming a single parent was hard to even imagine and very scary. I was not as worried about that, as I knew that Kris could do it, and that he would have a huge support system, both his family and mine. He would never be alone after I pass, and they would help him with our child and give that child an abundance of love. We decided that we would do it. We just needed to find someone to carry our child.

We talked through all the options and ultimately decided to work with an agency to help us find a surrogate and walk us along the path of surrogacy. My mom actually wanted to carry a child for us, but her health would be put at risk because of her age, and she was legally too old for surrogacy. Both my younger sisters, Cloude and Cozette, also wanted to help, but one was working on having their own child, and the other one had a newborn. According to the rules, you couldn't be a surrogate if you haven't had children of your own, so Tess was out. We also considered adoption, as it broke my heart to see so many children who needed to be adopted into loving homes. However, in order to adopt, you can't have a life-threatening disease, so we would not have qualified, which would have been another heartbreak. We had saved money to buy a house in the Bay Area and decided instead to use part of that money to hire an agency. We had heard from many others that that was the safest and smoothest way to go about it. Now after having done it, we totally agree!

We contacted Surrogate Parenting Solutions (SPS) and virtually met with the founder, since they are located in Orange County. We asked each one of the thousand questions we had, and let her know we needed time to think through everything before getting started. We also wanted to meet our fertility doctor and make sure our embryos were doing OK. The doctor said again that we probably just had a 7% chance of success per embryo; my age and the chemo I had back in 2008 lowered our chances. I still didn't believe that for a second as my eggs were really good grade, and if they were bad, we would have known already. I'm an optimist, and the doctor was clearly a pessimist. This was going to work! The problems I've had before with getting pregnant never had anything to do with the quality of my eggs. We decided to hire SPS, and they helped us understand the surrogacy rules in California. One of the more important questions about the legal aspect was — once the surrogate is pregnant, who, legally, are the parents? It was great to know that in California, compared to many other states that allow surrogacy, the intended parents, meaning us, would automatically be the parents to the child. We did not have to adopt our own child from the surrogate. This was great news, because I was terrified that because of my terminal illness, I wouldn't be allowed to adopt my own child. I envisioned it being a nightmare scenario. Thankfully, we did not have to worry about that.

We had to complete several questionnaires and forms. You name it, it was asked. Besides personal questions, there were some really tough questions that you had most likely never had to think about before. Like, for instance, would we keep the fetus if he/she had Down Syndrome or any other chromosome disorders, or terminate the pregnancy? All the forms we answered were used to match us with a surrogate that had similar values, a good match for us basically. The surrogate candidates answer similar questionnaires plus a lot of questions about how previous pregnancies went. Now we were on a waiting list to be matched with our perfect person with a perfect womb. We were told it could take four to six months to be matched with someone. So, we waited. The most important thing for us was to make sure we connected with someone on a personal level. We wanted to make sure we had a true connection with the person who would be carrying our child.

As we always did, we were going to spend Christmas in Ohio with Kris' family. I just love the Christmas celebrations we have there. Kris and I had been talking a little about whether we wanted to raise a child in San Francisco or if we should just leave the Bay Area when the time came. Since I wasn't working in Silicon Valley anymore, and with Kris being a finance guy who didn't really need to be in San Francisco for his career, we didn't have to stay in San Francisco. We knew we wanted to live in a house with a big yard, have access to good public schools, lots of green and nature, and have a safe environment for a child to just bike around or play outside with friends. We were now paying an arm and a leg for a tiny two-bedroom apartment, as we had moved back to the city again from Tiburon. We started wondering if it made sense to stay in the area once we had our baby. We weren't completely sure, so we decided to continue thinking about it and be open to exploring other cities to potentially move to at some point.

We had planned on doing a cross-country road trip to Ohio, to visit Kris' parents. There were so many places I still hadn't been to and would love to see, so we decided to drive by Austin, Nashville, New Orleans, the Grand Canyon, Antelope Canyon, Phoenix, and some other places along the way. It was such a fun trip. While we traveled through the different cities, we thought about if any of them would be a good candidate for our future home. They were all fun and beautiful, but we just didn't feel that special connection with any of them.

Life moved on, and I continued being tumor-free on my scans. It was an incredible feeling knowing there were no tumors growing and taking over my body. It didn't mean I didn't have cancer anymore; again, there is no cure for metastatic breast cancer, so the cancer cells will always be there. It is the constant treatment that MBC patients stay on that keeps it from growing. It's when the cancer cells become resistant to the treatment that new tumors show up or the ones that were stable before grow. Some treatments work for a very short time, others longer. It varies from person to person.

We were eagerly waiting to get matched with surrogates. Those four to six months felt like they took forever.

Finally it was our turn, and SPS sent us a couple surrogate profiles they believed were a good match for us. We reviewed and decided on one in July 2017. It was such a weird feeling to look at different profiles for someone who might carry our child. It felt a bit surreal. We met, had a great connection right away, and just talked and talked. We both agreed on moving forward, so the surrogate then had to do a few medical tests and a psychological evaluation. Everything checked out. All that remained was signing the contract, and we would be able to start the actual process. Unfortunately, at the same time, our surrogate had a big change in personal circumstances, which made the timing bad for the surrogacy. We decided to wait for another match. More waiting, but we are glad for it, because six months later in October 2017, we were matched with the most amazing surrogate mama. We were matched with Misha. It was love at first sight! She was awesome in every way. A super nice, strong, smart, and honest badass woman that does not take any bullshit: just my type of gal! We felt a great connection and instantly became friends. She has a super sweet and tough little girl and a very nice fiancé. After our meeting, we were so nervous as we definitely wanted to move forward with her but had no idea if she liked us as well. We met her on a Friday and had to wait the entire weekend to hear back from the agency that next Monday. We got great news — Misha liked us too, so we were a match!

We got all the administrative side of things completed, and Misha did all the tests. Her tests went well, and everything else turned out great. We then suffered with her as she had to go through all the hormonal injections to prepare her body for the pregnancy. The first week of February 2018, an ultrasound showed she was ready for our embryos. We decided to transfer two of the three embryos we had in the freezer, as two embryos would increase the chance of success. The transfer went well, and now came the excruciating wait. They call it the two-week-wait; it's literally a thing. You just cannot relax, you are climbing the walls, and of course time feels like it's crawling. We were living in a weird bubble of waiting. The news of whether or not Misha was pregnant couldn't come soon enough.

Misha went to the fertility clinic where she lives, in Roseville, to take the test. She told us we would get a call as soon as the results came in. We could hardly wait! Kris and I were holding each other on the coach when we got the call — *we are pregnant!* In fifteen years,

I had never received a positive result for a pregnancy test. This was the Holy Grail of the Holy Grail! We laughed, we cried. We were overjoyed! Finally, the statistics were on my side!!! Seven percent per embryo, that was the chance we had according to our fertility doctor. I'm just so happy we still went through with it, against all odds! Woohoooo!

The journey started. Over the next nine months, we did a lot of driving back and forth to Roseville from San Francisco. We were there for the ultrasound during week eight when we could hear the heartbeat — what a magical moment. The most beautiful sound in the universe. We went to several ultrasounds after that. We talked over the phone, sent little Marco Polo video messages to each other, and deepened our relationship. Misha was a rockstar. She had such an amazing attitude through all of it and was always fun to talk to. There was a lot of waiting, as nine months is a really long time. We kept a calendar on the wall that I would fill out with the weekly size of our little baby, what fruit or veggie he mostly resembled, size-wise, as well as all the different appointments and milestones.

The gender reveal was a funny story. We did a NIPT, Noninvasive prenatal testing, at ten weeks, which is basically a blood test where we found out if everything was OK with our baby's chromosomes. You can also with the same test find out the gender, so we sure did. We were way too curious, both of us. The process was that Misha would get the results mailed to her, since she is the one who was pregnant. So Misha wanted to do a fun gender reveal Marco Polo video message. First, we wanted her to just send the chromosome results to know that our baby was healthy. She texted an image of the healthy test results, but also, on it was a big blue gender symbol for boy. *Ahhhh, we were having a boy!!!* Misha had completely forgotten that the rest results also showed the gender on it. It took like two seconds and we got a text — *FUCK! I just ruined the gender reveal surprise, didn't I?* We just laughed out loud! We were having a BOY!

I would now be a boy mom. I always thought I would be a girl mom and teach my daughter to be a fierce feminist since I had fought so hard to free myself and become who I wanted to be. I loved it; now I would instead teach my boy to be a feminist, to always see women as equals no matter what, to look up to and have female role models. I would make sure he would empower his female friends and future colleagues when the time comes. I believe it starts when they are young. What we as parents teach them and what values we instill in them follow them for life. Also, I believe that when your kids only see mommy do all the household chores and take care of the kids, they will grow up thinking that's how it's supposed to be, and then another generation fails to move the needle forward for gender equality.

We loved visiting Misha and her family, getting to know each other, and strengthening our relationship over lunch and dinner. We were invited over to their Sunday Funday pool party hangout with their extended family. They were all so nice and welcoming. She let us get her headphones for her belly so we could record songs and stories for our baby boy and talk to him while he was growing inside her belly. She let us touch her belly and feel him kick. We just wanted to shower Misha with so much love. We are so immensely grateful for all she had to go through to give us this most precious gift. She will forever

193

be a superhero to us! Sure, she received money for doing this, but it is not the money that drives the surrogates hired by these agencies. First of all, one of the requirements is that they are doing well financially, so being a surrogate is done for other reasons. We learned that the surrogates who are part of this journey have altruistic motives. They do it because they want to help someone who is having a hard time with having a child. Each surrogate has a story as to why. We were so lucky that Misha came into our lives. Without her, we wouldn't have had the most precious gift of them all and the incredible injection of pure joy in our lives. Her act of love truly added years to my life.

# 28

# MOTHER AT LAST:
## A HAIRY CHILD IS BORN

In September 2018, one month before our baby was due, we had a big party — Baby Barney Shower Celebration and Farewell Party. We rented out the club room in our building and hosted a group of 150 people that included a mix of our close friends, work colleagues, and, of course, Misha. Even my oncologist was there. It was a great mix of people; everyone who had had a big part in our lives in the Bay Area. We wanted to have one last hurrah before our baby boy was born and before we moved away. My sister Tess and a friend helped out, and we went all out decorating the room with all kinds of blue baby shower things — there were balloons, banners, and garlands everywhere. My mom and sisters and friends in Sweden had surprised me with a traditional baby shower when we were visiting in Sweden earlier that summer, so this was our second celebration. But, I would have been happy to celebrate this time over and over. It was truly such a magical time. We had also received so many baby gifts from friends and family that one of our bedrooms in our apartment was filled with boxes of baby clothes and essentials. We didn't need to buy anything ourselves for the entire first year in our little boy's life.

The party was a success! It was wonderful to see everyone one last time before our big move. You see, when we found out we were having a baby, we decided to think more seriously about where our next home would be. None of the cities we had visited on our roadtrip during the winter of 2016 had felt right. We knew that we wanted to live in a place that was on the water, close to nature, and had a reasonable cost of living. We also wanted to live in a place that was family-oriented with good schools and was closer to Kris' family. We wanted to be on the east coast time zone, since that would make communicating with my family much easier than the nine-hour difference we had on the west coast. We checked out St. Petersburg and Tampa, Florida, as living on the beach sounded like a dream. We liked the area but realized that it might not be a good investment for the future, as the sea levels kept rising due to climate change, and the possibility of hurricanes there made it a risky choice. And honestly we just didn't feel that instant yes, this is home feeling when we visited. That had always been important to me, to feel connected to a place. I knew I would feel it in my heart when we found it. When we visited Cornelius on Lake Norman, twenty minutes north of Charlotte in North Carolina, we instantly got that feeling. We just loved the whole atmosphere and knew right away that this would be home. Kris had always talked about how he would like to check it out, as he had heard great things from friends who lived in the area. Plus, Charlotte is a big finance district, so it would be great from the standpoint of

Kris' career as well. I remember strolling in Jetton Park, which is a beautiful big park with a forest trail surrounded by the beautiful lake, and just falling in love. We could definitely see ourselves raising a child here. I could see myself pushing a stroller here, sitting at one of the beautiful benches facing the water, and just enjoying the serenity and beauty of the lake while holding my baby in my arms. We spent months checking Zillow ads to find our home, and sometime in late August, we finally found it. Even if we still had two months before our baby would arrive, we didn't want to go anywhere just in case he came early. We saw one house we were especially interested in after just seeing photos online. We asked our Realtor to take a virtual tour so we could take a "walk through" from a distance. We fell in love with this beautiful house that had a big yard, situated on the Peninsula in Cornelius. We put in an offer, and it was accepted! We bought a house, having never seen it in person, but we knew it was going to be perfect. Plus we were amazed, the 4,200-square-foot, gorgeous home cost less than a one bedroom condo in San Francisco. Quality of life was key for us, and we had found the perfect place for our little family.

So back to the baby celebration and farewell party. It was wonderful to get to say proper goodbyes and thank yous for the great memories and time we had had with all of our friends and colleagues. All of these amazing people had been part of such a big chapter in our lives, and a great support for us when I was diagnosed. It would be really sad to leave everyone, but many promises were made to make future visits and stay in touch. Several friends said hi to our baby and touched Misha's belly. I thought I would be sad because I wasn't the one carrying him, but I was actually OK. It had been such a long period between the time I first tried to have a baby back in 2003 and this day, that I was at peace with it. I had practically and emotionally accepted that I couldn't carry a child. I figured it was probably overrated anyways, I mean, most of my mom's friends had really tough pregnancies. I appreciated that Misha was OK with everyone touching her, especially us. She allowed us that special connection with our baby. Because of this, I had a better understanding of how dads feel. They don't connect physically with the baby before it arrives, but that doesn't mean they don't have a special connection. The only thing that really mattered was that we were having our baby boy, and Misha was doing well and felt great. She was definitely ready for the super active boy to come out though. It was all so amazing and magical — our dream was going to be coming true. I didn't have it in me at all to be sad about anything.

Our baby's due date was October 30, so I was a bit worried that he would come early and arrive on October 23, my birthday. I didn't want his birthday to be the same as mine, as I was thinking about the possible future when I was no longer here. However, Misha decided that she wanted to do a C-section, and we had, throughout the process, wanted her to drive all decisions concerning her body and health. We respected and were attentive to what she wanted.

We had a great handler from the surrogacy agency during the entire pregnancy. She managed everything between the three of us to make sure that everything went smoothly. She made sure Misha had all the support she needed, so we could focus on enjoying our time together and deepen our relationship throughout the nine months.

The C-section was scheduled for October 26, so on October 25 we packed our bag, installed the car seat, and headed to Roseville with feelings of excitement and unbelievable anticipation. We chose to stay at a hotel nearby the night before so we could get to the hospital as early as possible the next day even though the C-section wasn't scheduled until around noon. We had a wonderful dinner celebration with Misha and their sweet extended family. We came back to the hotel so excited that we couldn't sleep that whole night. We arrived super early the next morning. In fact, we were there before Misha, the one who was actually delivering our baby! We had already had a tour of where everything would take place and seen our rooms. We had chosen rooms next to each other, as we both wanted Misha to be close to us after the C-section.

They only allowed one person to be in the delivery room with Misha, so Kris agreed to watch through the glass so I could sit by her head as they delivered our baby. I stroked Misha's head, trying to soothe her with calm, loving words. I was probably more calming myself, since she was already very calm, and a badass like she had always been. Then I heard, "Here comes a hairy baby!" It all happened so fast, in just a few minutes. It felt surreal, he was here!? They took him to the table to be weighed and then let me cut the last of the cord that had already been mostly cut, but it still made me happy to get to do something. They said he was hairy because he had lanugo, just like I did when I was born! I cried and laughed — I was in such a euphoric state. I couldn't wait to hold him. I couldn't believe it — Alex was here!! He was beautiful and perfect! Hi, sweet baby — I am your *MAMMA!!*

Kris, our little Alex, and I were taken to our room so they could take care of Misha in the operating room. When we were finally in our room, we finally got to hold our baby boy. The three of us huddled together, and the two of us just stared at our little Alex. We held him skin-to-skin and alternated feeding him and holding him for the next 24 hours. We did not sleep a single second, we were just staring at him and making sure he was well-taken care of. Misha was doing OK and resting after the surgery. She pumped some breast milk for the first feedings, which was so wonderful of her to do. We were with him every second. We were with him when he had his first bath, and I held his little hand as he got his first shots and screamed at the top of his lungs. When Misha got to meet him and hold him, it was so magical and beautiful. We were so immensely grateful to her. My dream had finally come true. I was now a mother at last, and my life was complete!

When it was time for us to leave and take him home, we were super nervous. We couldn't believe they actually let us leave with him. We drove home so slowly that our two-hour drive home probably took four hours, as we drove way below the speed limit and kept stopping every ten miles or so to make sure he was doing OK, really just to hold him. It took us forever to get back to our apartment in the city. We left as a couple, and we came home as a family. Infinite joy!

# EMPOWERMENT IS WHAT REALLY DRIVES ME — WHAT DRIVES YOU?

Throughout my twenty-year career, I've been greatly motivated by empowering others to succeed — their success has been my success. Through my different professional roles, I've had the great opportunity to support startup entrepreneurs, innovators, innovation ecosystems — from science parks and incubators to cities and whole countries.

But why? I've been asked many times to use all that energy I have, those creative ideas, and great efforts to be part of initiatives that would make me rich and generate big exits, but I've chosen not to. It does not mean that I did not know my worth or got paid good money for my work. It just means that to really do a great job, my motivation had to come from something far more important than money or wealth. I have to feel like I'm doing something that's fun, engaging, challenging, and, above all, has a greater meaning and will help others to help themselves.

Sure, working with empowering innovation ecosystems might not seem that important to everyone, but to me it has been a way to move the needle forward in our world, helping people, cities, and countries to embrace innovation and use it to hopefully make our world a better place.

Empowering others has also helped me empower myself. It is a great reason as to why I've survived and thrived in life. Now, as someone who is on long-term disability for stage 4, metastatic breast cancer, I am thankful I can to continue empowering people, primarily others with metastatic disease. It is very therapeutic for me and gives me a great purpose in life. It also shows my son that his mamma did everything in her power to not die from this awful disease. Before I die, I want to make sure that I have done all I can to create more awareness and knowledge about metastatic breast cancer, and that I have raised as much funds as possible for research to discover new treatments. If not for me, then for the future women and men who will struggle with this horrific disease.

Ask yourself, what motivates you? Perhaps it's time for a change…

# 29

# SUBURBIA HERE WE COME: LEAVING MY OLD IDENTITY BEHIND

For the first two weeks after Alex was born, the three of us mostly stayed in our apartment. We went on a stroll or two around the neighborhood, but the air quality was so bad, as there were fires burning about an hour from where we lived. They may have been miles away, but you could still smell it and feel it in the air. Kris and I alternated taking care of Alex, feeding, and changing him. Since I obviously couldn't breastfeed him, he was on formula, so we were both able to feed him. That allowed us both to truly bond with him from the start. We just enjoyed life in our magical bubble, soaking it all in. We were so in love with this perfect little boy! My sister, Tess, and some of our closest friends came to visit and meet Alex during those two weeks. We had introduced him via video chat to both our families, and, of course, they instantly fell in love.

Kris had three months paid paternity leave after Alex was born, for which we were very grateful. Growing up in Sweden where both long maternity and paternity leave was a given, I was appalled when

I learned that most mothers in the U.S. were only given an average of four weeks of paid maternity leave, and fathers usually got none. We were therefore extra grateful to Kris' employer that had always been very supportive throughout our journey. In Sweden, parents are entitled to 480 days (sixteen months) of paid parental leave and get about 80% of their salary (with a cap), and some companies even pay their employees the difference. Most Swedish dads I know take at least six of those sixteen months. Also, the days don't expire until the child is eight years old.

During the two weeks of staying in our bubble, we packed up our apartment and got things prepared for our moving day. Luckily, living in such a small space meant we didn't have that many things to pack.

Before we left San Francisco, we had our first family photos taken by a very talented photographer, Christina, an old colleague and a good friend of mine. The smiles in the photos told the entire story. They were the smiles we had kept on our faces the first two weeks and the smiles that expressed the tremendous joy and love we had for having our precious Alex in our lives. We tried for hours to get photos of him with his eyes open, but that didn't happen. He just slept through the whole thing.

When it was time, the moving truck came and loaded up all of our belongings. It would take two weeks for the truck to arrive at our new home, so we flew to Ohio and planned to spend that time with Kris' parents before making the seven-hour drive to Cornelius.

They were so happy to finally get to cuddle with their brand-new grandson and spoil him rotten. At the time, Alex was the second grandchild in the Barney family, since Kris' brother Kurt and his wife

Rachel also had a little boy, Carson, who was then one and a half years old. Carson now has a little sister, Claire, who is the first and only female grandchild. The Barney family is known for producing mainly boys. As I'm writing this, we just welcomed Kris' younger brother Ken and his wife Lyra's little boy, Ryan. We are really happy that Alex has so many cousins on both sides of the family. My sister Cozette and her husband Wille have Adam, who is five and Lucy, who is one. Then we have my sister Cloude who has sixteen-year-old Vincent from a previous marriage, and with husband Andreas, she has four-year-old Bianca. We just wish we lived closer to all of them.

We soon realized we just couldn't wait two weeks. We so badly wanted to be in our new house and start our new life that we left Kris' parents after just one week. We had an air mattress delivered from Amazon, and we had some beach chairs, but that was about all we had until the moving truck arrived a week later.

We arrived at our beautiful home on Lake Norman and started our lives sleeping on the air mattress in the big living room, with so much gratitude and joy in our hearts. This is where we belonged. I could only hope that I would get to be here with my beautiful little family for a long time. I had now completely shifted my identity from a badass career woman to a suburban mom. Life was good.

# 30

## HOME AT LAST:
### THE PENINSULA ON LAKE NORMAN

From the very beginning, we knew we had made the right choice to move to the Peninsula in Cornelius. We loved living on Lake Norman in this very close-knit community. Kris and I left our old, fast-paced urban life with a hard focus on career behind and were now enjoying ourselves in suburbia where family, fun, and quality of life comes first. Our first year in our new home was wonderful, we enjoyed the precious time we had together seeing our baby boy grow and exploring our new surroundings. There is so much beauty around us with the lake and all the green scenery. Everything is so clean, serene, and pretty quiet compared to the hustle and bustle of a big city. We were also happy that we could walk outside without stepping into human feces. Sadly, that had become pretty common in San Francisco where homelessness was out of control. People who should have been taken care of in a mental health facility or drug recovery center were right outside your door, living in every corner or in tents on sidewalks all over the city. We did not miss that part of San Francisco! We had both loved the city so much the first years we lived there, but the problem just got worse and worse. The contrast between the rich and the poor was extreme.

We were so grateful for the sweet welcoming by our awesome neighbor who came by with a welcome basket and introduced us to other young families in the neighborhood. We had no idea what to expect, as we didn't know anyone on the north side of Charlotte; Kris had a couple of friends in the area, but they lived south of Charlotte. Being as social and outgoing of a person as I am, I just craved getting to know new people and making friends that we could hang out with. We had no idea before we moved here, but luckily our area is a very popular one amongst transplants, meaning people like us who moved here from other parts of the country. Most had moved from big cities on the coasts. I had been worried that we would be one of the few young families as we had moved to a community with a golf course and a country club, but it turned out there were plenty of young families like us. I had also thought that since we were somewhat in the South that I would, as a pretty liberal person, not find like-minded people. Thankfully, I was totally wrong. I became friends with the most amazing group of women, now my girl tribe, as they've declared themselves, and Kris became friends with their husbands. Luckily, since 95% of us were transplants that had recently moved in and didn't know anyone, we all craved new friendships. Perfect! Having friends and a social life has always been very important to me. We've all grown close, and in addition to having fun together, being out on the lake, hanging out at the pool, sharing meals together, and doing activities with the kids together, they have become a huge support system for us while we go through all the hardships that come with living with a deadly disease. My new awesome girl tribe brings over meals, drives me to appointments, showers me with fun little surprises, and is just an amazing support, letting me vent and cry when I need it. I just love them so much for it! Especially since my loved ones are so far away.

# 31

## LIVING LIFE LIKE THERE IS NO TOMORROW
### AND LIKE I'M GONNA LIVE FOREVER

We easily settled into our new life in North Carolina. Everything was perfect. After the best three months ever, Kris' paternity leave was over, and he had to go back to work. The good news was that he had a short commute — just upstairs to his office in our home! It was wonderful that we would all still be home together. We hired an absolutely amazing nanny, Cherie, who helped take care of Alex part time. I wanted to spend all the time I possibly could with Alex, but it tired me out so much if I took complete care of him the entire day. I deal with tough side effects every day, from nausea and pain to just overall fatigue. It doesn't matter how much you sleep, with fatigue like I experience, you have unexplained, persistent, and relapsing exhaustion after just being active for a couple of hours. I didn't want to be constantly exhausted when I spent time with Alex; instead, I wanted the time I spent with him to be fun and active. I wanted to enjoy every precious second we had together and create beautiful memories.

When we moved here, I started going to a brand-new cancer center, Wake Forest Baptist Comprehensive Cancer Center, about an hour drive from where we live. As a new patient who needed several different doctors, I had several appointments a week to meet with a specialist for each issue. Metastatic breast cancer patients have many issues due to side effects from treatments, and therefore we have way too many doctors. I was lucky that my oncologist at UCSF referred me to an old university friend of hers, another badass female oncologist that I right away felt was right for me. It is very important to have the right oncologist for your care, someone who will be your champion and make sure you get the best care and most groundbreaking treatments possible. Someone who is not just your doctor, but who actually cares about you and wants the best for you as well. I've heard so many nightmare stories about lousy oncologists through my mets sisters, support group friends that also have metastatic breast cancer. Our disease is a life and death situation, every single treatment we are put on is crucial, and it is important that our oncologist is well aware of what treatments are out there that would work with our specific subtype. Our oncologist should be the last one to give up on us. Our oncologist is also the one who refers us to the specialists we need for our different side effects and overall damage from the disease and treatments.

Since Kris and I have always loved to travel, we said early on that we would keep traveling even after having Alex. He's been on many flights by now, around six round trips. Two of them have been to

Sweden. In the Summer of 2019, I went to Sweden for four weeks with Alex, and Kris joined us about two weeks later. We had a wonderful, typical Swedish summer, enjoying the beauty of Stockholm and the archipelago with my family. We also hung out with all my closest friends and their families. It was a wonderful feeling to finally have my own kid. All these years, my friends had all had children, some two and even three, and I had always been the one without. I was always immensely happy for them and never ever felt any bitterness or resentment, I just don't have it in me. I love every single one of their kids, and of course especially my best friend Jessica's girl, Olivia, my goddaughter. It was amazing when it was time for our annual group photo, that I, for the first time in all these years, stood there as a mother holding my child. Epic! We let Alex stay with my parents for a few nights so Kris and I could go to Paris for a romantic get-away. It was AMAZING, and even if we missed Alex a lot, we were able to just relax and enjoy our alone time in beautiful Paris.

I want to make sure that Alex has a really close relationship with my parents, siblings, and his cousins, so my plan pre-Covid was that we would spend at least four weeks every year in Sweden. I asked my sister Cozette, his godmother, that when I pass away, if she could be his Swedish mamma and continue the tradition. She accepted, even though no one in my family ever wants to hear about me dying. However, it is important to me that I have made my wishes clear no matter if I die next year or five years or longer from now.

I am also glad that Kris and I can cry together and talk about dying and what's going to happen when I'm no longer here. He also knows my wishes about my final moments, my funeral, etc. I actually want to have a memorial while I'm still alive, as the last thing before I pass. I want to gather all my family and friends, my loved ones, and have a last hurrah farewell party! Haha! I know it sounds sick, but hey, it's my dying wish. I don't want people to grieve my death, I want them to celebrate my life with me before I leave it. I want us to share memories and laugh about them together, dance and sing my favorite songs. I've also let Kris know my weird wish that I want my ashes to be spread in space, even if it's just where the Earth's atmosphere stops and outer space begins. I've reached out to an acquaintance in Silicon Valley who is on Space-X's board of directors and told him my wish. I really hope they can make it happen. I want to be one with the stars, and for my loved ones to look up at the night sky and know that I'm right there looking back. I will also want to have some kind of memorial headstone both in the U.S. and in Sweden. I know, I have many demands for my passing, but luckily I have time to make it happen before I take my last breath. Death is unfortunately our reality, and it is important for us that we can talk about it with our loved ones.

Just while writing this today, I checked my social media and saw the sad news that yet another mets sister has passed away, another young mother in her thirties with little ones. So many have died in our online support group for young women with MBC, just these past few weeks. Our reality is devastating. Every time it happens, it is a constant reminder that we are carrying a disease that will kill us, and that our time on this Earth is very limited. And we wonder, who is next? Is it me? I have several times thought that maybe it's better if I'm not part of any support groups for MBC, to not be constantly reminded of my mortality, but then I think these incredible women and few men are the only ones who really truly know what I'm going through. They can help me deal with things in a way that no one else can. And I also personally like being there and helping others.

So back to living life. The same year as the Paris trip, we celebrated Christmas in Sweden with my family. I had not done that since before I moved to the U.S. in 2011. It was wonderful to introduce Kris and Alex to the Swedish Christmas traditions, and some Syrian ones too. Again, Kris and I left Alex with my parents and flew to Northern Sweden, above the Arctic Circle to stay at the ICE Hotel in Jukkasjärvi. It was a magical experience! We had four amazing days, doing all kinds of snow-related activities like a dog sled tour with beautiful huskies, snowmobile ride looking for the Northern Lights, visiting with the indigenous Sami and petting their reindeer, among other things. The most epic experience, however, was spending a night at the ICE HOTEL and sleeping in an ice artsuite. It's the world's first hotel completely made of snow and ice. The ice comes from the Arctic Torne River, Sweden's largest national river. The annual hotel is built over twelve weeks in the late fall and melts back to the river in April. Artists from all over the world compete to be selected to sculpt an Art Suite. All of the artwork done in ice was incredible. The rooms in 2019 represented nature, everything from the jungle to the Serengeti with animals and their natural habitat sculpted into pieces of ice and snow art. We slept in a suite called "a cabin in the woods." It was so cool; everything was made of ice, but we got to sleep in sleeping bags that can handle really cold temperatures. You only wear thermals, a hat and gloves, and very warm socks. The only thing sticking out of the sleeping bag is your face, so you notice when you wake up that your face is all icy, because your breath condenses in the cold air and creates tiny droplets that eventually freeze. The only thing that sucked was when you felt that you needed to pee in the middle of the night…

As I wrote earlier, I was really sad that Covid put a stop to our six-month mini around-the-world trip. I really hope that I get to do the trips on my bucket list before my time is up. My absolute top ones are the Safari in Africa and New Zealand North-South Roadtrip.

Since my diagnosis of metastatic breast cancer almost five and a half years ago, I have had a body scan every three months. Every three months, I don't know if my life is going to come to an end sooner or later. We call it "scanxiety." In early 2019, my scan showed that Ibrance, the treatment that had kept me tumor-free/progression-free for over three years had stopped working. That meant the cancer cells became resistant to it. The scan showed that I had a progression in my femur and had to go through more SBRT radiosurgery. This procedure caused significant damage in my hip bone, which means a hip replacement surgery is definitely in my future. I was also put on a new oral treatment called Verzenio in combination with Faslodex. Faslodex is given as injections that you get monthly in each butt cheek, and it hurts like hell!

This treatment had much tougher side effects, but it worked well for a while. Just six months after starting the new treatment, I was tumor-free again. However, my last quarterly scan on July 15, 2020 showed that I had three new tumors in my femoral neck. Since my third line of treatment stopped working, it is time to get on the fourth one, Piqray. In addition to more radiation, surgery is part of the treatment sometime down the line. I am starting to run out of options, but I still have hope. Hope that new treatments keep being approved or more treatments are available through clinical trials. These are only possible if more of the pink fundraising efforts are focused on research for metastatic breast cancer. I will tell you all about the importance of advocacy and MBC campaigning at the end of the book.

Despite having lived a life with cancer as the annoying roommate that buts into everything, the daily intake of twenty pills with horrible side effects, the scars from the surgeries I have had so far, and knowing that death is lurking around the corner, I have had and still have an absolutely amazing life. I truly love my life so much. I feel it from my head to my toes, and I have zero regrets.

I am so grateful for all the kindness, compassion, and support from all of my loved ones. There is, however, one person who is by far my number one rock — the love of my life, my husband, Kris. I'm incredibly grateful and feel lucky to have such an amazing man in my life. He helps me navigate this awful disease to make sure that we are not missing anything crucial. He is my partner in all the decisions about treatments, surgeries, you name it. He holds my hand through the excruciating procedures, and he lets me cry in his arms when I need it. He is strong for me when I need it, and I am strong for him when he needs it, as we are both going through this. Add to that, he is an amazing father and is always present in his son's life. We take care of our child and home equally, so Alex knows that he can call for both of us about everything. When mommy is resting because

WHEN LIFE HANDS YOU CACTUSES, MAKE MARGARITAS

her treatments are kicking her ass or not home, daddy has everything under control, and they are having the best time together. I never have to worry about that, and THAT is always a good thing, but becomes even more important when you live with a deadly disease and know your time is limited. I love him so much it hurts. He knows that I want him to continue having a wonderful life even after I pass. I want him to find love again and continue experiencing life's beautiful moments with that person. Even if it breaks my heart, and I'm already now jealous that Alex will have a new mamma, I know that Kris would only choose someone who would treat him and his son in the best possible way. OK, enough crying, I'm still here…

My hope is that I will release the second edition of this book several years from now to share the stories of the many adventures, wonderful experiences, and the fun times I have had with my Kris, sweet Alex, and my awesome family and friends over the next five-plus years of my life. I don't take any moment in life for granted. I take everything in. Everything. I don't want to blink for fear of missing something. I want to make sure I max out the Bank of Joy and Memories before I leave this world. I try to take a lot of pictures and film everything I do with Alex so he will always have special memories to hold onto. My wish is that I keep my promise to my baby boy that I will see him grow up to become a wonderful man. I do realize it is statistically unlikely that I will be here when he is grown. My first goal is to see him celebrate his fifth birthday. That is three years from now, October 26, 2023. Will I still be here? I hope so! Let's make a date, I'll see you on my Instagram @adibabarney on that date, say, "Yay, you're here!" in the comment, and I'll know you saw this and were with me in hoping and praying for this day. Every time someone mentions any kind of future, it is hard not to always think, *will I still be here?* or get sad because it is far in the future, and most likely I won't.

No matter how much time I have left with my loved ones, with my heart and soul, Alex, min toksnok, my silly goose, I want him to know me and to know my story. I want him to know how I yearned for him for so many years and how overjoyed I was the day he was born and he made me a mamma (Swedish for mom). I want him to know that I love him more than the sun and the moon and all the stars in the sky. I love him with all my heart times infinity. He is the reason I finally finished this book.

But for now... I'm living life like there is no tomorrow and like I'm gonna live forever.

# LEAVING A DENT:
## MAKING AN IMPACT

$\int$ ince I only have so much energy because of the constant tough side effects from my cancer treatments, I told myself that I would not focus on anything but my little boy for his whole first year. No advocacy or any volunteer work, just my little family and making a life for us in our new home. So I completely disappeared from the advocacy scene and chose to excuse myself from all of my board assignments.

I was honored to receive the HERS Breast Cancer Foundation's "Empowerment Award 2016" and Susan G. Komen's "Make A Difference Award 2017" for my advocacy work in the Bay Area.

When Alex turned one, we started him in preschool, as we wanted him to learn and socialize with other children his age. It was now time for me to start doing advocacy work again.

I had heard about this great non-profit organization that focused 100% of their efforts on metastatic breast cancer called METAvivor, so I applied to be a volunteer. METAvivor is the only organization of its kind that guarantees that 100% of every donation and 100% of the proceeds from every fundraiser (after event expenses) goes into metastatic breast cancer research grants. Most of us volunteers at METAvivor are metastatic breast cancer patients. Mostly women, but also a few men who are all champions, working tirelessly to make a difference. I was so happy that I had learned about them, as it fit perfectly with my own mission. I desperately needed to get back to fighting for our cause. I was passionate and fierce about making some kind of change for those of us who live with metastatic breast cancer (MBC). I started thinking about putting on a big fundraising gala similar to the successful Metsquerades that have been put on in several cities around the U.S. My plan was that the gala would take place at our country club, The Peninsula Club, that has a beautiful space for that type of event. I created a project plan and was just about to get a team of volunteers together to start the planning work when news of Covid started coming in.

As I mentioned earlier, we feel invisible in the pink ribbon campaigns, since a lot of the awareness campaigns out there during the pinkmania/pinktober are focused on early detection and breast cancer in general. Therefore, there is always a great need to create more awareness around metastatic breast cancer, educating the public about this disease and how it is to live with it. In fact, since most of us had early stage breast cancer before being diagnosed with stage 4, MBC (like I mentioned earlier, about 30% of breast cancer survivors will eventually get diagnosed with MBC, even years after completed and successful treatment), each of us can say with 100% certainty that MBC is like a whole different disease and world compared to earlier stages of breast cancer. First of all, our world is far from rosy pink. In fact, METAvivor created a three-colored ribbon for us metavivors to highlight the uniqueness of the disease and show its commonality with other stage 4 cancers. The base ribbon is green and teal to represent metastasis. Green represents the triumph of spring over winter, life over death, and symbolizes renewal, hope, and immortality, while teal symbolizes healing and spirituality. The thin pink ribbon overlay signifies that the metastatic cancer originated in the breast. Second of all, our stage is not curable, we will die from it. We will also always be in treatment; there is no end or finish to our treatment plan. When one treatment stops working, we have a progression due to the cancer cells becoming resistant — we move onto the next one and next one until there are no more treatments available, and then we die. There are very big differences between the early stages and our stage 4. When you hear that someone died from breast cancer, they actually die from metastatic breast cancer since early stage breast cancer doesn't kill. Why this is not communicated is beyond me. Not even the breast cancer foundations around the world in their constant "every day this many die of breast cancer" fundraising campaigns mention that "this many die of metastatic breast cancer," not breast cancer; there is a huge difference, and words are important. Knowledge is power!

My personal awareness campaign, #knowmbc, has been running on social media for a great part of 2020 and gained a lot of attention. It's a campaign where I have shared facts about metastatic breast cancer for 100 days leading up to my 43rd birthday on October 23, 2020. Facts that you normally don't hear during the pink ribbon campaigns. The raw and honest truth about living with this deadly disease. All the facts can be found on facebook.com/knowmbc.

I'm also helping out with another awareness campaign organized by moorefightmoorestrong and METAvivor called #LightUPMBC that lights up landmarks in all 50 states in the U.S. and other countries around the world with the colors teal, green, and pink on October 13, which is the official Metastatic Breast Cancer Awareness Day. By lighting up these landmarks, we put the focus on MBC, telling our stories and raising funds for research. We need more funding for research, as research means more treatments that will allow us to live longer. Please, amazing readers, think about where your pink donations go. Ask when you purchase a pink ribbon-branded product, "How much goes to this cause? Where does the money go?" and "What is it being used for?" In fact, why not just skip that altogether and donate to research, as that is the only thing that can make a real change. I, of course, support all foundations that help people struggling with breast cancer, no matter what stage, and don't want to take away from those efforts. I am, however, very much against all the pinkwashing out there where tons of products are branded as a pink ribbon product, when they're in fact not, not even informing their customers about what the donations go to. They are basically just making money on our suffering.

Besides the awareness campaigns and fundraising efforts, I also help out with advocacy, as I feel like there is so much unfairness in the U.S. healthcare system. There are so many people out there who can't afford the new effective treatments due to their insurance being lacking or because they might not even have insurance. Does that mean that they have to die? Should income or wealth determine if we live or die? Since earlier chemo was only available as infusion in a clinic, the cost for treatment was considered the same as a medical visit. Now, with more and more new cancer treatments and chemo becoming available as pills, the treatments are considered pharmaceutical. So, for patients who don't have adequate insurance, these new drugs are not affordable at all, and the patients die because they can't get access to the latest treatments. The oral treatments I've been on for the last four years would have cost me $10,000–$15,000 a month if my insurance didn't cover it. As advocates, we are constantly trying to change this and many other issues. We want to make sure that everyone, with no exception, has access to the latest and greatest care, and has the same chance as everyone else to live longer and be there for their families. We also want to make sure they have access to disability pay and insurance, no matter their income or wealth. I, unfortunately, know way too many people who can't afford to stop working, as they wouldn't have access to any support. We also want to make sure that the governments keep investing in cancer research. We have to put an end to this disease that is killing more than 600,000 MBC patients every year around the world. If not cure it, let's at least make it into a chronic illness instead of the deadly disease it is now.

I also want my son to know that his mamma did everything in her power to not die from this horrific disease. Before I die, I want to make sure that I have done all I can to create more awareness and knowledge about metastatic breast cancer, and that I have raised as much funds as possible for research into new treatments. If not for me, then for the future women and men struggling with this horrific disease.

# THANK YOU FROM THE BOTTOM OF MY HEART

First of all, I want to give a huge thank you to a wonderful woman that has helped me make this book a reality. A brilliant author that has added her magical touch to my story and packaged my words beautifully in this book. Ellen Bryant Lloyd, I have enjoyed every single second we have worked together on this book project. I am so grateful to StoryTerrace for connecting us. Big thank you to StoryTerrace and Natalie Rose for all your support in making my book a reality. Furthermore, I want to give special thanks to the talented Angie at Jacoby Rose Photography for the beautiful cover photos, and the very creative and brilliant designer, Heather Strianese, at Leveret Paperie for the beautiful cover design.

Thank you to all who have read my book, for letting me share my life story with you. As I mentioned in the beginning, I decided to write this book for me, my son, and for you. Putting my story on paper has been a wonderful reminder for me to always cherish and celebrate every moment I have in my life before it is over.

I love that Alex will grow up knowing my story in full and have my words to comfort him on tough days. It brings me joy knowing he will always be able to hold his mamma close in his heart through these pages. He will know just how much and deeply I will always love him, even when I'm no longer here.

My hope for you, my friends, family, and readers from all over the world, is that my words touch you in a way that inspires and empowers you to live your life to the fullest, no matter what. To be resilient and confident. To love fully and deeply. To push through fear and let it motivate you to truly live. To let go of the things that don't matter. To completely embrace your amazing journey on Earth. Life is precious, make the best of it.

May you thrive. Always.

Love,

Adiba

# JOIN ME AS MY STORY CONTINUES...

Add me on Instagram @adibabarney and follow me on Facebook (my personal Adiba Barney and my awareness Knowmbc page) to read more about my life and to see the special events of my life documented in photos, both from my past and as they continue to unfold. After all, I am an open book. :)

I hope that my posts will highlight many more years of my life being lived with joy and laughter, mixed in with the challenges that come with a deadly disease.

By purchasing this book, you are contributing to Metastatic Breast Cancer research and helping to make an actual difference in the lives of many. Ten percent of the profits go to METAvivor, and the rest are put aside in a fund for my son Alex, when he grows up, to continue supporting the metastatic breast cancer community and of course research, in his mamma's honor.

I sourced my facts about Metastatic Breast Cancer from:

METAvivor.org
Breastcancer.org
Cancer.org
Cancer.gov

And my Swedish facts from:
Sweden.se

# 20 FACTS ABOUT METASTATIC BREAST CANCER